Sunset

COMPLETE
TILE

by Steve Cory and the Editors of Sunset Books
Menlo Park, California

SUNSET BOOKS

Vice President and General Manager: Richard A. Smeby

Vice President and Editorial Director: Bob Doyle

Production Director: Lory Day

Manufacturing Director: Rosann Sutherland

Art Director: Vasken Guiragossian

Staff for this book:

Managing Editor: Bridget Biscotti Bradley

Writer: Steve Cory

Art Director: Amy Gonzalez

Photography Director and Stylist: Cynthia Del Fava

Text Editor: Esther Ferington

Illustrator: Anthony Davis

Page Production: Linda Bouchard

Proofreader: Audrey Mak

Prepress Coordinator: Eligio Hernandez

Indexer: Nanette Cardon

Cover: Design by Vasken Guiragossian and
Jackie Mancuso. Photography by James Carrier.

10 9 8 7

First printing May 2002

ISBN: 0-376-01678-7

Library of Congress Control Number: 2001095006

Printed in the United States.

For additional copies of *Complete Tile* or any other Sunset book,
call 1-800-526-5111 or visit us at www.sunsetbooks.com.

C O N T E N T S

TILING POSSIBILITIES

For thousands of years, people have responded to the lasting beauty of tile. Ceramic and stone tiles that were set centuries ago still possess a welcoming sheen and a classic beauty. Newer products, such as porcelain and glass tile, share and even improve on the ancient qualities of durability and ease of care. Vinyl and wood tile, although not as long-lasting, offer a softer surface and additional design options.

Installing tile was once a specialized task best left to professionals. But the advent of easy-to-use materials, such as backerboard, thinset mortar, and organic mastic, has put most tiling jobs within the reach of do-it-yourselfers. Tiling, however, is not a job to be taken lightly; there are many opportunities for mistakes that are all but impossible to correct. This book helps you steer clear of those mistakes, and shows you how to install tile surfaces that are every bit as smooth, straight, and durable as those set by professionals.

How to Use This Book

Complete Tile begins with a chapter that introduces the variety of available tiles. Even if you think you already know which tile you want, take a look at the possibilities; you may change your mind. Before you buy your tiles, make sure to look at the portions of the book describing your project, to understand how you will install the tiles.

The next chapter describes the tools and materials needed for most projects. Later chapters show specialized tools for specific projects. Be sure to have all the tools and materials you need before you start a project.

The following four chapters tackle the four basic types of tile installations—floors, walls, countertops, and outdoor patio surfaces. Each of these chapters begins with a gallery of finished projects, to get your creative juices flowing, and then gets down to business. In each chapter, preliminary directions tell you how to prepare a substrate that is strong and smooth enough for the tile, and how best to lay out the job. Detailed instructions for individual projects follow. You'll find complete step-by-step directions for a wide variety of tile installations.

A final chapter presents techniques—some tried and true, some using the latest technology—for making tile and grout look as fresh as the day they were installed. This chapter covers the most common repairs as well.

Hiring a Pro

If you don't plan to take on a tiling job yourself, use this book to become an educated consumer. Read through the first two chapters to familiarize yourself with the available materials. Then read the relevant sections for your project in the later chapters to find out how the substrate should be prepared and the tiles installed.

Ask a tile setter for references from previous jobs, and visit the sites where the work was done if possible. Work up a contract that deals with particulars—substrate preparation, tile-setting materials and techniques, and finishing touches such as moldings or bullnose tiles. A pro may set tiles in a mortar bed—a technique that is not recommended for amateurs, but that produces a very strong installation.

Discuss with the tile setter how level and straight you expect the tiles to be. No tile installation is perfect, but with most materials a professional can achieve consistent and straight grout lines, and a tile surface that is not bumpy. Tile setters working with materials such as limestone or Mexican pavers, however, do not aim at precision; imperfection adds to the rustic charm.

WATCH THAT BACK!

Even if you never lift anything that is particularly heavy, a few hours spent on your knees or bent over, troweling adhesive and setting tiles, can wreak havoc on your lower back. You may not even feel any pain as you work, but may awaken the next day in agony. Especially if you are not used to this kind of work, take it easy. Arrange the work site so that you are as comfortable as possible. Lift with your legs, not your back. Take plenty of breaks; stand up and stretch out. And enlist help to lift something heavy.

SELECTING TILE

Let your imagination run wild when it comes to choosing tile colors, sizes, and styles, but don't neglect the practicalities. If the area to be tiled will get wet, either choose tiles that repel water, or be prepared for some extra maintenance. Select floor tiles with a grainy or bumpy surface, so they will not be slippery when wet. While any tile is strong enough for a wall, make sure floor tiles are extra strong.

Choose the whole ensemble. For a wall, look not only for field tiles (the ones in the middle of the wall), but also for endcaps and corners (see page 115). When selecting floor tiles, choose thresholds and base moldings to harmonize. In the case of a countertop, plan for several types of trim tiles (see page 152). Trim tiles are usually more expensive than field tiles; be sure to include them in your budget.

This chapter organizes tiles by material—ceramic, stone, porcelain, and so on. With the rise of modern manufacturing methods, however, many tile materials have become chameleon-like. Porcelain or ceramic tiles, for instance, can be made to look like natural stone (either smooth or textured) or even terra-cotta. Chances are you can get the look you want as well as the tile properties you need.

In this pattern, each 8-inch field tile has one corner cut at an angle; four cut-outs accommodate a square accent tile. The field and accent tiles look like saltillos, but are actually glazed ceramic.

FLOOR TILES

Ceramic and stone floor tiles must be stronger than wall tiles. (Tiles for countertops must be nearly as strong as floor tiles.) If your dealer cannot assure you that a tile will be sturdy enough for your purposes, see if it has been rated for strength, perhaps by the American National Standards Institute (ANSI) or the Porcelain Enamel Institute (PEI). Unless you expect extra-heavy traffic, your tiles need to be approved only for residential, not commercial, use.

Floor tiles are often thicker than wall tiles. Preparing the substrate and installing thick tiles may raise the floor more than ¾ inch above an adjacent floor surface (see pages 60–61); if so, you may want to select a thinner tile such as porcelain or quarry tile.

Traditionally, ceramic and stone floor tiles have been of five distinct types: glazed, quarry, polished stone, rough stone, and terra-cotta. But newer cement-body, ceramic, and porcelain tiles can be made to look like any of these. To add to the happy confusion, some tiles made from glass and even metal are strong enough for floors.

For a softer floor surface, choose among vinyl, rubber, wood parquet, or even cork. These materials are also an ideal choice if the floor is not strong enough for ceramic tile.

Glazed Ceramic Tile

Ceramic glaze is a glass-like material that is baked onto the tile, so that it bonds firmly to give the tile a hard, protective shell. Glazing makes possible a dazzling variety of color choices. People often choose a floor that recedes visually, but if you want your floor to grab some attention, use bright glazed tiles, perhaps in a checkerboard or other pattern.

A common misperception is that all glazed tiles are too slippery for wet areas. But makers of floor tiles often employ techniques to make a skid-resistant glazed surface. The tile body may be textured, or the glaze itself may have a bumpy surface.

To endure years of foot traffic, a tile's glaze must be both very hard and very resistant to abrasion. Check with your dealer to be sure that the glazed tiles you choose will withstand abuse.

These glazed ceramic tiles look like natural stone—they even vary in color from tile to tile—but are easier to maintain.

Some porcelain tiles are colored on the surface only; if you chip a surface-glazed tile, another color and texture is revealed. Through body porcelain tiles have a uniform color running all the way through, so a chip is far less obvious.

Porcelain Tile

Porcelain is made by firing fine, white clay at extremely high temperatures. The result is a tile that is amazingly tough—either impervious or at least vitreous (see page 9). Porcelain tile is nearly impossible to stain.

Many older bathroom floors were tiled with 1-inch-wide hexagonal porcelain tiles. Until recently, it was not practical to make large porcelain tiles, but the development of the monopressatura (single-layer) method has made it possible to manufacture large porcelain tiles. They are usually similar in cost to glazed ceramic tiles.

Because porcelain starts out pure white, it can be tinted to just about any color. And because the tiles are produced in a press, they can take on just about any texture. Porcelain tiles may be made to closely resemble tumbled or polished marble, travertine, quarry tile, limestone, ceramic tile, or even terra-cotta.

While some feel that porcelain tile is an imperfect replica, lacking the true texture and natural beauty of stone or ceramic tile, others swear by porcelain's tremendous ease of cleaning and excellent stain resistance.

Quarry Tile

Although quarry tiles were originally made of cut stone, today's tiles of that name have never been near a quarry. Instead, they are made using an extrusion process, which produces a ribbed pattern on the back. Quarry tiles are unglazed, so they bear a resemblance to tiles cut from stone.

Because they lack a glazed surface, quarry tiles may be prone to stain. Vitreous types are more stain-resistant than semi-vitreous tiles (see page 9). Applying a sealer can solve this problem.

Unglazed tiles like these are often recommended for floors, because they are not slippery when wet; even when sealer has been used, a small amount of moisture spilled on quarry tiles will soak in, rather than bead up. Special non-skid quarry tiles have a pattern of raised dots.

Because quarry tiles are made from red clay, color choices are more limited than for porcelain pavers. Earth tones, grays, off-whites, and pastels are the most available options.

HARDWOOD TILE

Tiles made of resin-impregnated wood offer exciting design possibilities, and they are installed much like ceramic tiles. Lay them in thinset mortar, and fill the joints with latex-or epoxy-reinforced grout. Consult with your dealer to choose both mortar and grout.

Colors include wood tones, pastels, and earthy hues. Most are interestingly mottled and streaked; no two tiles are exactly alike.

These tiles are stronger, more stable, and better able to withstand moisture than wood parquet tiles (see page 20). Yet they retain some features of wood: they are warmer to the touch and a bit more flexible than ceramic tiles, so that dropped glasses are less likely to break.

Cement-Body Tile

Most tiles are made by firing clay at high temperatures. Cement-body tiles are completely different in that they are actually little slabs of concrete.

Concrete can be stained to any color, in tones that range from pastel to bright. Some concrete tiles take on the veined appearance of marble; others have solid colors. The tile surfaces can be rough and porous, or shiny and fairly resistant to moisture.

Cement-body tiles are often the most economical choice. They are tough enough to hold up for many years. And you may find some of the more adventurous colors and textures enchanting.

But there are drawbacks: though durable, cement-body tiles stain easily unless regularly coated with a sealer. The more porous types should not be installed in areas that will get wet. Check with the manufacturer before installing these tiles outdoors, because some types will crack in freezing weather.

Decorative Floor Tiles

Many floors are covered with tiles that are all the same shape and size. This simple plan is often best, since much of a floor will be covered with furniture or rugs. But if a floor will be a focal point, consider jazzing it up with a pattern or small splashes of color.

It's usually preferable to lay a large pattern or use widely spaced accent tiles; small designs over a large area can look fussy. To lay intricate designs in a small area, consider mosaic floor tiles (see page 17).

Colored "dots" are most often small squares laid at an angle, for a diamond shape. If a dot occurs at each corner joint, buy octagonal tiles designed to be used along with the dots. If fewer dots will be used—you may choose to scatter them more or less randomly, and perhaps use several colors—you may need to cut the corners of some large tiles.

Large rectangular decorative sections are usually placed in the middle of the floor. Consult closely with your tile dealer when planning a pattern. If the pattern requires you to cut tiles to fit, the cuts will need to be very precise.

Setting occasional accent tiles usually calls for cutting out notches in the field tiles. Again, these cuts need to be precise; consider having the tile supplier make the cuts for you.

Spaced two tiles apart, decorative floor tiles make a big impact on this white ceramic floor. The same tiles were used on a colorful backsplash.

Decorative tiles may have geometric or floral designs, or may simply be glazed with a dramatic color.

Dark green polished marble tile with a sinewy veined pattern contrasts strongly and beautifully with white wainscoting and bathroom fixtures.

Natural Stone Tile

Except for polished granite tiles, natural stone tiles absorb stains with distressing ease, and can be difficult to clean. But for many people, nothing else quite matches the variegated patterns and deep beauty of real stone. And with regular care, even the most porous stone can last for generations.

Most stone tiles are cut as precisely as ceramic tiles. However, because they are natural products, no two stone tiles are exactly alike. For a more uniform appearance, make sure all your tiles are from the same color lot, and buy plenty of extra tiles. Stone tiles from the same box may vary significantly in color.

Traditionally, stone tiles have been polished to a shiny surface that repels moisture. Recently, tumbled marble and granite, which have a nearly sponge-like appearance (see page 145), have become popular. Various stone tiles may also be "honed," "resplit," or even "sandblasted," for a softer look and a rougher surface. These tiles are especially in need of a sealer.

Marble: Characterized by deep or light veins that can vary dramatically from tile to tile, marble has long been associated with wealth and luxury. Today, however, it is possible to find a selection of reasonably-priced marble tiles at home centers as well as specialty tile stores.

Not all marble tile is created equal. Some types are very soft, so they are easily scratched and easily stained. Others are fairly hard and easier to keep clean, but all marble should be sealed if you expect spills or scuffs. If a tile dealer cannot tell you how soft a marble tile is, make a test on a scrap piece. Run a key or other piece of pointed metal lightly across it, and see if a scratch results.

Granite: Much harder and denser than marble, granite usually is speckled or mottled rather than veined. Commonly rated as vitreous, granite can be used for countertops and areas subject to prolonged exposure to moisture.

Some types display almost whimsical specks of color against a cream background, while darker granite tiles take on a somber, European style look.

Onyx: Tiles made of onyx display swirls and clouds of light and dark browns. They are both expensive and soft, so choose them only if you fall in love with the look.

Travertine: In addition to fine veins and mottled color, travertine is characterized by small, scattered pits on the surface. The tiles tend to be fairly soft, and the pits soak up moisture and stains. But the warm, tan hues and soft feel may make it worth the extra maintenance. Some travertine tiles also come with the pits filled with similar-colored grout, for somewhat easier maintenance.

Quartzite: Notable for their pebbly surface, quartzite tiles are nearly as hard and stain-resistant as granite, making them a good choice for floors. However, they are expensive and often difficult to find.

GRANITE

TRAVERTINE

GRANITE

ONYX

GRANITE

AGGLOMERATED STONE TILE

At a tile store or home center, you may find inexpensive stone tiles with a jumbled appearance, as if various stones have been mashed together. These may be mislabeled "marble," but they are actually agglomerate tiles, made by recycling leftover stone materials. The result is often interesting and attractive, though these tiles are usually as soft as marble.

Limestone: Until recently, people would not have considered installing rough, open-grained stone anywhere but on the outside of a building. But newly popular techniques such as tumbling and sandblasting (see page 14), actually seek to mimic the appearance of rough-cut stone. So why not install the real thing?

Limestone tiles (left) tend to be large, thick slabs. Some are not precisely cut. Colors run from cream to brown, often spiced with flecks of darker material. Limestone installations frequently emphasize the rustic nature of the material: rough tile edges are exposed, the surface may be a bit uneven, and the grout lines may not be of consistent widths.

Of all the stone tiles, limestone is the most porous. Sealing after installation is mandatory; unsealed limestone will almost certainly develop hard-to-remove stains.

Slate: Traditionally, slate (below) has been produced by splitting rather than cutting, followed by polishing the surface. The result is a highly textured surface that is resistant to moisture. Because of this, it is often used outdoors and in bathrooms. Harder than limestone and darker in color, slate has also been a popular choice for hallways and vestibules. Colors run to grays, greens, black, and reddish brown. Recently, slate that has been cut and left unpolished has gained in popularity. These tiles are almost as porous as limestone, so be sure to seal them.

Mosaic Floor Tile

When you see a floor tiled with hundreds of little squares or hexagons, chances are the installation was easier than it looks. Some professionals occasionally install tiny tiles one at a time, just as it was done in ancient times. But much more commonly, pros and homeowners use mosaic tile—sets of small tiles that come bonded together on a mesh backing.

Mosaics are available for just about any tile material—ceramic, polished stone, rough stone, and porcelain. The tiles may be all the same color, or several complementary shades may be scattered more or less at random. A mosaic tile floor is slip-resistant even if the tiles are glazed, because there are so many grout lines.

Stunning mosaic floor patterns, many made in Italy or Spain, add spice to a floor for little effort. The cost per square foot is high, but it takes only a small section to add a great deal of visual interest. Mosaics made of cut and polished pebbles have a hand-laid look.

Most mosaics come in rectangular sheets, often 12 inches square. Individual tiles may be as small as ¾ inch square or as large as 4 inches square. If you need to remove some of the tiles from a sheet, simply slice through the backing (shown at right) with a knife. Sheets can be laid next to each other for a seamless appearance, even if the individual tiles are not rectangular.

You can also buy large tiles made to look like mosaic sheets. The "grout lines" on these are glazed along with the rest of the tile, so that installing is less work and the resulting surface is easier to maintain.

A large area—both floor and walls—covered by tiny mosaics gives the impression of a pixellated digital screen, throwing the cabinets and countertop into sharp relief.

Resilient Tile

Tile that "gives" a little may not be as solid as ceramic or stone tile, but it has a key advantage. If you drop a plate on a resilient floor, it has a chance of surviving unchipped.

Vinyl and rubber tile: Most resilient tile is made of vinyl composition (that is, vinyl mixed with tiny stones and other resins). "Solid vinyl" tiles are about 90 percent vinyl, which makes them more durable and resilient than vinyl composition tiles. Rubber tiles are the most durable, but are available in only a small range of colors.

Vinyl or vinyl composition tiles have flecks of various colors, to hide dirt. The color runs all the way through the tile. Tiles of these types must be sealed regularly, or dirt and grime will work deep into the tiles. Some come pre-waxed. Avoid solid-color vinyl tiles; they are nearly impossible to keep clean.

These tiles are often called "commercial tile," and are used in grocery stores, schools, and other high-traffic places. When mixed together to make a checkerboard or a playful pattern, commercial tile is not only practical, it can be downright cheery. See pages 80–85 for installation instructions.

A checkerboard pattern makes inexpensive vinyl tiles look good. Here, a combination of reds and earthtones lends a warm glow to a breakfast nook.

Surface-printed tile: Many resilient tiles have a pattern printed on the surface only. Some are stamped to mimic brick, wood, or ceramic tiles, while others display floral or geometric patterns.

Most surface-printed tiles have a no-wax finish, which resists moisture and dirt effectively. However, don't expect the finish to last forever. When the no-wax surface wears out, apply a special no-wax conditioner.

Cushioned surface-printed tiles have a foam backing. Avoid these, because they can be damaged when you move an appliance or even when you slide a chair while sitting in it.

Purchase self-stick tiles with caution; some have unreliable adhesives. Many pros apply adhesive to the floor for added grip.

Bright blue surface-printed resilient tile is a great choice for a busy kitchen. The speckled pattern hides dirt well.

CORK TILE

This old-fashioned material is making a modest comeback. Natural cork retains a slight springiness for decades, so it is a forgiving surface for those who suffer aches and pains from hard floors. Install cork using a special cork tile adhesive, and protect the surface with regular applications of wax or sealer.

sturdy, no-wax finish. High-quality tiles fit together so well that there is no need to seal the joints; once installed, the floor only needs to be wiped clean.

The special adhesive for these tiles can be surprisingly expensive, so don't neglect to take it into account when pricing out the job.

Most parquet tiles can be cut into quarters by slicing through the mesh backing with a knife. To cut the wood itself, use a circular saw or saber saw. See pages 87–89 for installation instructions.

Polished parquet tiles provide a warm background for lush, pink drapes.

Wood Parquet Tile

For centuries, wood parquet floors composed of hundreds or even thousands of small pieces were proudly displayed in the homes of the wealthy. Creating these floors required painstaking labor by skilled craftsmen. Today, a homeowner can easily install inexpensive machine-made parquet tiles that achieve a very similar look.

At a home center or tile store you will find parquet tiles in a range of materials and shades. Oak is the most common wood used. Some tiles are made of maple or birch; others may be cryptically described as "hardwood," which is likely to mean ash or poplar. The wood may be stained lightly, or given a dark, mahogany-like appearance.

Before you buy parquet tiles, pull out a few and check them for quality. Each tile should hold together well—usually, via a mesh backing. If the tiles fall apart easily, installing them may be difficult. When the tiles are laid on a flat surface, there should be no gaps between them. Slide several pieces together, and see that the tongue-and-groove joints are tight. Most parquet tiles have a

Laminate Tile

Laminate strip flooring (often referred to by the brand name Pergo, though there are many manufacturers) is similar in composition to a laminate countertop, although the flooring usually has a wood-grain design. Strip flooring is easy to install, wipes clean in a flash, and resists dents. Recently, manufacturers have also been making laminate flooring in tile form. Individual pieces fit together in tongue-and-groove fashion, just like wood parquet. Pages 90–93 show how to install laminate tiles.

These durable and easy-to-clean laminate tiles are laid in a modified herringbone pattern using square accents.

Terra-cotta Tile

Unglazed tiles in earthy colors are generally referred to as terra-cotta. Most are a light reddish brown, but some are much darker, and others take on yellow and gray tones. Unless the surface has been tinted, the color runs through the body of the tile.

Terra-cotta means "baked earth," which neatly sums up the simple way these tiles are made. A tile's hue depends on the clay of which it is composed. Tiles from different countries, such as Mexico, France, Italy, or Portugal, have distinctive coloring. But you may find significant color variation among tiles from the same area—even tiles packed in the same box. This natural variability adds to the charm of a terra-cotta floor.

Terra-cotta tiles are nonvitreous, and readily soak up water. They need to be sealed to protect against staining, and should not be used outdoors in freezing climates.

Just about any throw rug looks great on a backdrop of outdoorsy saltillo tiles. Octagonal tiles on the stair risers add visual interest.

You'll find terra-cotta tiles in various shapes: square, octagonal, hexagonal, and rectangular with pointed ends. They are often laid in interlocking patterns that use tiles of two or more shapes and sizes. Small dots of different-colored tile may be laid in a regular pattern, or scattered randomly. You can even incorporate hand-painted art tiles into a design.

Some terra-cotta tiles are machine-made, and can be laid in the same way as most other ceramic tiles. Many, however, are hand-made and have irregular shapes. See pages 166–169 for instructions on laying these.

Handmade Mexican saltillo tiles are particularly rough-textured and uneven in shape; you can expect chips at the edges and small craters in the surface. Some saltillos come coated with a thin clear "glaze." Don't trust the glaze alone to protect the tile.

In a room that embraces weathered imperfections, unglazed and irregularly shaped tiles are the perfect complement.

SEALING UNGLAZED TILES

Unglazed tiles that are nonvitreous should be sealed to protect against stains. A tile dealer can help you choose the best sealer for your tile. Generally, there are two options. "Surface" or "film-forming" sealers penetrate only slightly into a tile, and produce a shiny surface that repels moisture. Most have a satin rather than a glossy sheen, but you may not like the way they darken the tile. "Penetrating" sealers soak deeper into the tile, and do not change its appearance as much. However, they don't protect as well as surface sealers.

A wood threshold creates a smooth transition between tumbled limestone tile and carpet.

Thresholds: If the new tiled floor comes in at the same height as an adjoining hardwood or carpeted floor, you may not need a threshold. Cut the tiles so that they form a perfectly straight line parallel to the edge of the adjacent floor, and fill the gap with grout. Usually, however, a threshold is needed to resolve a difference in height between two abutting floors.

Select a threshold that harmonizes with both the tiles and the adjacent floor. A metal threshold that sits on top of the tiles is easy to install and covers up imperfections in the tile edges, but it will also collect dirt and may be a tripping hazard. A wood or marble threshold installed on the same substrate as the tiled floor is much more attractive and easier to clean. You'll need to cut the abutting tiles precisely, however, because their edges will show. See pages 92–93 for installation instructions.

Thresholds and Baseboards

Attractive thresholds and baseboards do a lot to enhance the final appearance of a tile floor. Choose among the options for each ahead of time, and incorporate your plans into the layout for the job.

Baseboard options: To trim out a floor with minimal effort, reinstall the wood baseboard previously on the wall or install vinyl cove base. You may want to paint the wood base before reattaching it.

For a more substantial look, consider creating a wall base using tiles instead. Bullnose tiles of the same color as the floor make for a seamless look. Contrasting bullnose tiles add definition to a room. Pieces of granite or marble can also make a handsome base. Just make sure that the top edge of the tile or stone base is finished, because it will be highly visible and will need frequent cleaning.

CHOOSING GROUT

Depending on its color, grout can drastically change a floor's appearance, or it may blend in so that it is hardly noticeable. If a grout color contrasts strongly with the tile, the tile shapes are emphasized, creating a geometric effect. If grout nearly matches the tile's color, the floor will look more like a unified whole. Tile stores and some home centers offer grout samples (right), so you can see which grout looks best with your tile.

If you choose a contrasting grout and you want a neat appearance, your grouting must be done to near perfection. All the lines must be consistent, and all the corners crisp. This can be difficult, if not impossible, to achieve if the tiles are at all irregular. Of course, if you're aiming for a rustic appearance, imperfect grout lines are not a problem.

Grout lines may be as narrow as $\frac{1}{16}$ inch or as wide as $\frac{1}{2}$ inch. Before planning your layout, place loose tiles on a surface that is nearly the same color as the grout, and experiment with different widths to see which looks best. Use unsanded grout for lines less than $\frac{1}{8}$ inch wide, and sanded grout for lines that are $\frac{1}{8}$ inch wide or wider.

Grout should be sealed within a week or two of installation, or it will be easily stained. Use a special grout sealer (see page 183).

Unless the grout is polymer- or latex-reinforced, mix it with liquid latex rather than water. For a countertop or other area that needs to be very resistant to stains, consider using epoxy grout.

WALL TILES

Because they do not need to be as strong as floor tiles, wall tiles are often less expensive, and they come in a wider choice of colors. Traditionally, wall tiles have usually been about 4 inches square. Today, however, people install just about any size and type of tile on a wall, including floor tiles and stone tiles. Just make sure you can get the trim pieces you need; otherwise, you will be left with unfinished edges.

Most wall tiles can be cut on a straight line with a snap cutter. A rod saw blade attached to a hacksaw can be used to make curved cuts and cutouts. Check with your dealer to be sure of the correct cutting method for the tile you choose.

Glazed Ceramic Wall Tile

The most common type of wall tile, glazed ceramic, has a soft, nonvitreous body covered with a glaze. The glaze on wall tile is not as tough as that on a floor tile, but it effectively seals out moisture. If an area will be subject to scratches, choose a tile with a glaze that is hard enough for countertops. (Don't install wall tile on a floor or countertop.)

A rainbow of colors is available. In addition to solid-colored tiles with a smooth, glossy surface, wall tiles may be textured to resemble rough stone; crackled, with a crazed pattern of tiny cracks; variegated in color; or glazed to appear as if they were hand-painted with a brush. Most wall tiles are stocked with border and bullnose trim pieces to match (see page 31).

Don't be afraid to make up your own design using tiles of different colors. But if you do, buy tiles from the same manufacturer, to be certain they will be exactly the same size. Most ceramic wall tiles are self-spacing; small nubs along each side ensure that when the tiles are butted together a gap of about ¼ inch automatically appears. Installing tiles that are not self-spacing takes a bit more time and patience.

Metal Tile

Metal tiles don't just have a metallic finish; they're actually made of copper, stainless steel, brass, or even iron. Beautiful but expensive and difficult to cut, they are usually used as occasional accents, such as in the tiled kitchen backsplash and hood shown above. Some types may rust or discolor if exposed to moisture.

Glass Tile

Correctly installed, glass tiles are strong enough for most wall installations. (Some types are even installed on floors.) They can be nearly transparent, almost totally opaque, milky, or smoky. Colors may be pastel or bright. Available textures include glassy, pebbly, and craggy. Glass is by nature impervious to moisture, so these tiles are ideal for areas that get wet.

Depending on the glass tile's texture, you may be able to install them with organic mastic, latex-reinforced thinset mortar, or epoxy thinset. Whichever adhesive you choose, make sure it's white; gray or brown adhesive will muddy the color. Consult with your dealer to find the best grout.

Mosaic Wall Tile

For the greatest variety of colors and shapes, take a look at mosaic wall tiles. In addition to arrays of squares and hexagons similar to mosaic floor tiles (see page 17), wall mosaics may combine several splashy colors, or have crazy-quilt designs. Some of these are expensive, but they are no more difficult to install. Mosaic tiles may be glazed ceramic, stone, or porcelain.

Tile stores also carry circular, rectangular, and geometric mosaics that can be used as decorative features. By the square foot they are expensive, but it takes only a small section to liven up a wall. In addition to the mosaics on display, a tile store may have catalogs you can leaf through. Some decorative sections fit into a tile job easily; others may require that you custom-fit the surrounding tile.

Mosaics are the best choice when you want to tile over a curved wall surface. The smaller the individual tile, the neater the job will look.

If you have the time, consider making your own mosaic pattern, using shards of broken tile. Page 175 shows how to do this on outdoor stepping-stones, but the same method can be used for a wall.

A one-of-a-kind quilt effect (above) is achieved by mixing and matching segments from several types of mosaic sheets. A mosaic border (below) can be purchased in ready-assembled sections.

A shower niche created from narrow slate tiles (left) has almost a rainbow effect. Polished travertine tiles with pinstripes of marble mosaics (below) give this bathroom a crisp, clean look.

Stone Wall Tile

Marble, granite, limestone, slate, and other stone tiles commonly used on floors (see pages 14–16) can also be used on walls. Depending on the material and the texture, stone wall tiles may be formal or rustic, smooth or rough. With its swirls, veins, and speckles, natural stone renders a wall fascinating as well as beautiful.

Although they are sometimes expensive, polished marble and granite tiles can be priced reasonably; check several tile stores and home centers. These tiles must be laid precisely, because any imperfections will be very apparent. If the wall is flat, however, installing them is within the reach of a careful do-it-yourselfer. Where a tile's edge will be exposed, you can pay a contractor to polish it, try polishing softer stone yourself (see page 136), or cut the tile with a wet saw and apply clear lacquer to the edge.

Rougher stone tiles have less stringent installation requirements; in fact, unevenness is often considered appealing. Typically, exposed edges are not finished.

Art Tiles

It only takes a few art tiles to make a dull wall exciting. Tiles with raised or painted designs can powerfully evoke another time and place. Tiles depicting animals, plants, or celestial objects spur the imagination of children and adults alike.

Many art tiles, especially those with painted designs, have non-vitreous bodies and soft glazes that can be scratched easily. Others—often, those with raised patterns—are made of sterner stuff. Consult with your tile dealer to be sure how durable the tiles you buy are. Few art tiles are strong enough to be used for a countertop or floor.

Carefully plan how and where art tiles will fit into a tiled wall. If they are exactly the same size as the other tiles, just make sure to position them pleasingly (see page 111). But if they are different sizes, you'll probably need to cut the surrounding tiles.

Two handpainted art tiles flank this bowl sink. The tile edges are finished with thick grout for a rustic look.

Borders and Trim

Trim tiles finish off a tiled surface's exposed edges, giving the job a professional look. Borders act like a picture frame to define space and separate one section of tiles from another.

The most common trim tiles are bullnose pieces, which have one edge that curves into the wall. A "surface bullnose" tile is like a regular flat tile with one edge rounded over. A "radius bullnose" tile has a more radical curve, so that the body of the tile must rest on a surface—usually, a piece of backerboard or a mortar bed—that is raised above the surrounding surface (see page 149). An outside corner requires a special corner tile, with a bullnose edge on two sides. Bullnose tiles may be the same size as the field tiles, or they may be narrower and longer—typically, 2 inches by 6 inches.

Countertops have special trim tile requirements, to cover the front edge of the counter as well as the backsplash. Pages 138–145 show some of the possible configurations.

Borders are available both in single tiles and mosaic sheets. A border may be as wide as 4 inches or as narrow as ¼ inch. Often, a wide border is installed along with thin border pieces directly above and below it. Some border pieces have finished edges, so they can be used as trim tiles as well. A border may run horizontally only, or it may also extend vertically to complete a picture frame effect.

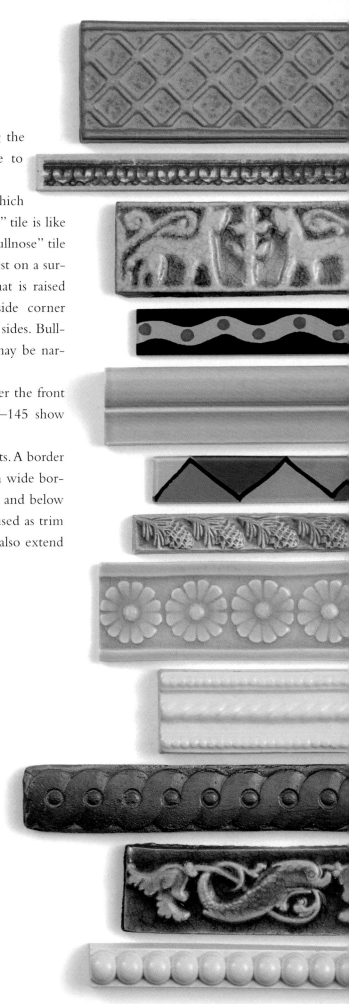

MAKING YOUR OWN

You may live near a ceramics craft store, where customers can hand-paint designs on tiles. Often, children make the most charming designs. The tiles are then fired, covered with a clear glaze, and fired again. The result is usually a nonvitreous tile with a fairly soft glaze, equal in quality to many factory-made tiles. Be sure to find out what size the tiles will be after they have been fired.

TOOLS & MATERIALS

For tiles to be laid firmly and evenly, it is imperative to have the correct tools and materials. If you apply the right adhesive using a properly sized notched trowel, for instance, you'll find it easy to install tiles that stick and form a smooth surface. With the wrong trowel or adhesive, even the most experienced tile setter would struggle to produce a satisfactory job.

Fortunately, gathering the right stuff is usually simple and inexpensive. In addition to standard household carpentry tools, you will probably need no more than seven or eight hand tools, and perhaps a rented wet saw.

Tile jobs usually involve five basic operations: preparing the substrate, laying out the job, cutting tiles, setting tiles, and applying grout and caulk. This chapter presents a basic tool kit for each operation.

Buy materials at the same time as you buy the tiles; a salesperson should be able to tell you how much of each material you will need. If the surface to be tiled is already firm and flat, you may need only adhesive and grout. If the surface is imperfect, however, you may need to buy substrate materials and perhaps a membrane as well.

TOOLS OF THE TRADE

A homeowner usually doesn't need expensive, contractor-grade tools. On the other hand, you should avoid bargain-bin tools, which may not be accurate or well-made and can be hard to use. Mid-priced tools sold at a home center are often the right choice.

In many cases, you may already have the tools you need on hand. For demolition work, often the first step in a tiling project, you're almost certain to have something to do the job. A hammer and a stiff, straight-bladed paint scraper or a putty knife are usually best for removing old tiles and scraping away adhesive. Use a flat prybar for heavier demolition.

Tools for Preparing Substrate

Before laying tiles, it is often necessary to install an underlayment of cement backerboard, plywood, or greenboard. Less often, the structure of a floor or wall needs to be strengthened; a modest collection of carpentry tools will enable you to handle most of this work.

Drill with screwdriver bit

A ³⁄₈-inch variable-speed, reversible drill is powerful enough to drive screws to anchor backerboard or greenboard. Buy a magnetic sleeve and several #2 Phillips screwdriver bits designed to fit it. This will enable you to drive screws more quickly than you can pound nails.

Drywall square

Designed for use with drywall, this large tool makes quick work of measuring and marking cement backerboard, plywood, or greenboard.

Knives

A standard utility knife is the best tool for cutting greenboard. It will also cut backerboard, but the going will be tough; a special cement-backerboard knife (above) is faster and easier to use. A grinder with a masonry or diamond blade (see page 37) cuts underlayment quickly, but also spews plenty of dust.

Layout Tools

A successful tile installation starts with working lines that are straight, square, and, in the case of walls, plumb or level. Accurate measuring and marking tools are essential to getting the job done right. For a typical residential installation, a tape measure, square, level, chalk line, and perhaps a straightedge are all that's needed, although a layout stick can help with a difficult job.

Jury stick

Also called a layout stick, this tool eases the task of laying out a complicated floor or wall. You can make one on the job site using a straight board and a pencil; follow the directions on page 68.

Level

A carpenter's level, also called a spirit level, tells you if a line is plumb or level. To check a level for accuracy, place it on a flat surface and note the position of the bubble. Flip it upside-down; if the bubble is in exactly the same place, the level is accurate. Some levels have adjustable bubble vials. If you cannot correct an inaccurate level, replace it.

Chalk line and straightedge

A taut string makes a perfectly straight line; with a chalk line, you can mark that line on a floor or wall. (See page 69 for how a chalk line works.) Use a straight-edge to mark a line or to check tiles for straightness. Tile setters use aluminum straightedges of various sizes, but a metal carpenter's level or the factory edge of a sheet of plywood also works fine.

Square and tape measure

Use a carpenter's square, also known as a framing square, to see if two lines are perpendicular. To make sure a square is accurate, set it on a flat floor against a wall, positioning the square so that its tongue (the short side) rests on the floor and faces left along the wall. Scribe a line on the wall. Flip the square so the tongue faces right, and scribe a second line. If the two lines are not parallel, the square is inaccurate; replace it. A 25-foot tape measure is the best measuring tool. Check that the hook slides back and forth slightly, so that inside and outside measurements will come out the same.

Tools for Cutting Tile

Most wall tiles can be cut with hand tools—a snap cutter for straight cuts, and nippers or a rod saw for curved cuts and cutouts. For making straight or curved cuts in floor tiles, consult the chart on page 186. To cut round holes, use a drill with a masonry bit, or a hole saw. See pages 70–71 for further instructions on how to use some of the most common tile-cutting tools.

Tile nippers

Also called biters or a nibbling tool, a pair of tile nippers can take a bite out of almost any tile. To make a cutout with nippers, you must be patient and careful; it's very possible that you will break a tile or two in the process. But if you have only a few such cuts to make, this tool could save you the trouble of renting a wet saw. Nippers are also useful when you need to shave less than ½ inch from a tile. Score the line with a snap cutter, and chip away with the nippers.

Snap cutter

Most tiles can be quickly cut along a straight line using this inexpensive tool. Check that your snap cutter is large enough for the tiles you need to cut. It should have an adjustable guide to ease the job of cutting several tiles all the same size. Better models have replaceable blades, also called scoring wheels.

Hacksaw frame with rod saw blade

If you're working with a soft tile, a hacksaw equipped with a cylindrical rod saw can cut curves and cutouts. Use a clamp and a scrap of wood to hold the tile still while you cut.

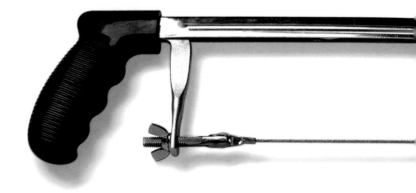

Tile stone

Tile stones come in handy on several occasions. If cutting a tile results in a sharp or jagged edge, rub it with a tile stone to round the edge a bit. You can also use a tile stone to grind down a soft tile that is ⅛ inch or so too large. If soft unglazed tiles (such as terra-cotta, saltillo, or limestone) form an uneven surface, grind down the high spots with a tile stone, a process called "lipping."

Grinder

A grinder cuts quickly through any type of ceramic or stone tile, but it kicks up plenty of dust as it cuts, and makes precise cuts with difficulty. A grinder is ideal for tight cutouts, such as a hole for an electrical receptacle or wall switch. Equip it with an inexpensive masonry blade if you are cutting soft tiles or have only a few cuts to make. To make more than a few cuts in hard tiles, consider investing in a diamond blade.

Wet saw

A wet tile-cutting saw produces precise, clean cuts. With it, you can even cut ¼-inch-wide slivers out of most types of tile. Water sprays continuously onto the diamond blade, preventing the blade from wearing out. Adjustable guides make it possible to produce cuts at 45 degrees or other angles. Unless you plan to take on several tile jobs, rent rather than buy a wet saw.

INEXPENSIVE WET SAWS

Some wet saws cost little more than the price of a two-day rental. Be judicious about purchasing one, however. The diamond blade will be of lower quality than the one in a typical rental saw, so it will wear out quickly if you cut very hard tile such as porcelain. Before you buy a model with a sliding tray, make sure it is large enough to handle your tiles, and test to see that you can easily make accurate cuts. A hand-held model is the least expensive option of all, but it can be difficult to use, especially if you need to make precise cuts.

Tools for Setting Tile

To set tile properly in thinset mortar, you must mix the mortar so it is free of lumps; see page 73 for more information on how to mix mortar with a paddle attachment like one of those shown at right. Organic mastic for wall tile does not have to be mixed. Either type of adhesive must then be spread to form a flat surface with consistent notch lines. Finally, you'll need to tap the tiles so they stick to the adhesive and form a flat surface.

Trowels

Choose trowels with thick, comfortable handles made of wood or rubber. Examine the blades to make sure they are straight, and see that none of the teeth on a notched trowel are bent. Buy a notched trowel to match the job—usually, a V-notched trowel for wall tiles, and a trowel with square-cut notches for floor tiles. The thicker the tile, the deeper the notches must be. A margin trowel (right), which looks a bit like an egg turner, is a great general-purpose tool. Use it to mix mortar, to back-butter tiles in tight spots, and to scrape away excess mortar and grout.

Mixing paddles

Very small amounts of thinset mortar can be mixed by hand, but for most jobs you'll thank yourself for buying a mixing paddle. For an average-sized job, a small paddle designed to be used with a $\frac{3}{8}$-inch drill will do, as long as the drill is strong. For mixing larger amounts, rent a $\frac{1}{2}$-inch drill and buy or rent a large mixing paddle.

Mallet and beater board

To tap tiles into place, use a beater board, also called a beating block—a flat piece of wood about 5 by 10 inches in size. It is best to lay the board directly on top of the tiles; covering the board with cloth or carpet makes it less precise. Tap the board lightly with a rubber mallet. For large tiles, especially if they are irregularly shaped, use the mallet by itself.

Finishing Tools

Grout lines of consistent width and depth are essential to a neat-looking job. With a few simple tools and some attention to detail, you can achieve a satisfying and attractive result.

Caulking gun

For most jobs, a standard-sized caulking gun, which uses 10-ounce tubes of caulk, is just fine. If you need to caulk many feet of wide joints, consider buying a large caulking gun that uses 1-quart tubes.

Wiping tools

Always have a bucket and a large sponge on hand to wipe the tiled surface after grouting. A wet towel can make the job go faster on a floor. To clean away grout or mortar that has hardened, use a scrubbing tool with a fiberglass mesh pad; anything harsher might scratch the tiles. Be sure to have a faucet or hose handy, so you can change the water in the bucket often.

Striking tools

If you have trouble creating consistent grout lines using a sponge, consider running a tool that is slightly concave along the lines, a process called striking. Depending on the width and desired depth of the grout line, you could use a pencil eraser, a tool handle, or an official striking tool called a jointer (above).

Laminated grout float

Purchase a grout float with a face that is laminated with hard rubber. After using the float to press grout into place, the hard rubber surface acts like a squeegee.

TILING MATERIALS

The materials that lie hidden behind tile determine whether the tile will last for centuries or only weeks. A stable, firm subfloor; flat and even underlayment; adhesive that grabs hard and long; and long-lasting grout all contribute to a pleasing and durable tile job.

Underlayment Options

If a wall or floor is solid, it may be possible to tile directly over it. However, if the existing surface is not strong enough, or if the area will get wet, install materials designed specifically to support tile and, in some cases, to withstand moisture.

Cement backerboard: Some pros install tile the old-fashioned way, by pouring a thick slab of mortar and setting the tiles directly in it—a time-consuming operation that requires special skill. Today, homeowners can achieve the same moisture tolerance and strength by attaching sheets of cement backerboard.

Cement backerboard comes in two varieties, both made primarily of Portland cement, which retains its strength even when it is soaked with water. Fibrous cement backerboard has fibers running throughout its body, and is smoother. Mesh-reinforced cement backerboard is basically a slab of cement held together by an embedded fiberglass mesh that wraps around both sides; this board has one very rough side and one that is fairly smooth but pitted. Both types are available in thicknesses ranging from ¼-inch to ⅝-inch, and in sheets of various sizes.

Attach either type of cement backerboard using special backerboard screws, which are strong and can easily be

FIBROUS CEMENT BACKERBOARD

MESH-REINFORCED CEMENT BACKERBOARD

driven flush with the surface of the board. Standard drywall screws are much more difficult to drive flush, and are prone to break. Drive the screws using a drill equipped with a screwdriver bit. Seal joints between pieces of backerboard with fiberglass mesh tape and thinset mortar.

Greenboard: Also called blueboard, greenboard is drywall designed to withstand moderate amounts of moisture. It is less expensive and easier to install than cement backerboard, but not nearly as durable; if water seeps through even a small gap at an edge or a seam, greenboard will crumble in time. Use it only where tile will not get very wet—for example, on bathroom walls that do not surround a tub or shower.

Plywood: Plywood is the best underlayment for non-ceramic flooring such as vinyl tile, cork, wood parquet, and laminate tiles. It is inexpensive, easy to cut and install, and can form a very smooth surface—an important consideration when applying thin resilient tiles that show every imperfection in the subfloor. Plywood designed for underlayment has a series of cross-shaped marks, which makes it easy to drive screws or nails in a grid pattern.

Ceramic or stone floor tile can also be installed on plywood, as long as the floor structure is firm and the tiles will not get very wet. If moisture is an issue, it is best to install ceramic and stone tiles on cement backerboard, as plywood will swell when wet.

CHOOSING THE RIGHT UNDERLAYMENT

TYPE OF TILE	RECOMMENDED UNDERLAYMENT
Ceramic or stone floor or countertop tile	Cement backerboard
Ceramic or stone wall tile, fairly dry location	Cement backerboard or greenboard
Ceramic or stone wall tile, wet location	Cement backerboard
Resilient floor tile	Plywood

GREENBOARD

STANDARD PLYWOOD

PLYWOOD UNDERLAYMENT

Membranes

Two situations call for the installation of a membrane: extreme moisture, or a substrate that may shift or crack. If a floor or wall is likely to become very wet, water can eventually seep through the grout and even through concrete backerboard, damaging the wooden flooring or framing behind it. A waterproofing membrane avoids the problem and protects a home's structure. If a floor substrate is likely to crack or shift slightly over the years, an isolation membrane can prevent cracks from transferring through to the tile or grout.

Membrane materials: Older installations often used roofing felt as a membrane; today, polyethylene is more common for most applications. For floors that will be exposed to standing water for prolonged periods, use a professional-quality waterproofing membrane. Many types are composed of two layers, one fibrous and the other made of modified bitumen. To get maximum protection against cracks, use an isolation membrane composed of a layer of polymer and a reinforced fiber sheet.

Trowel-applied and sheet membranes: Any membrane must firmly bond with the substrate, using either paste or mortar.

A "trowel-applied" membrane comes in two parts, the membrane and the adhesive or paste. One type has a temporary paper backing; see page 64 for installation instructions.

Paste is also used with a type of membrane, used for cracks only, that consists of a narrow roll of mesh tape. Spread the paste with a trowel, roller, or brush, roll the mesh onto the paste, and apply another coat of paste. When the paste dries, you're ready to tile.

A "sheet membrane" is applied in much the same way, except that it is set in thinset mortar rather than adhesive. Trowel the thinset onto the floor using a notched trowel, and roll the sheet membrane onto the thinset. Allow it to set; then apply another layer of thinset and set the tiles.

Membranes for walls: If a family uses the shower for hours a day, moisture can seep through the grout and the backerboard to damage wall studs. Protect the framing by stapling a membrane to the studs before installing the backerboard. Roofing felt (also called tarpaper) is an ideal product for this purpose, because it is impregnated with tar, which partially seals around staples and nails that are driven through it. See page 121 for installation instructions.

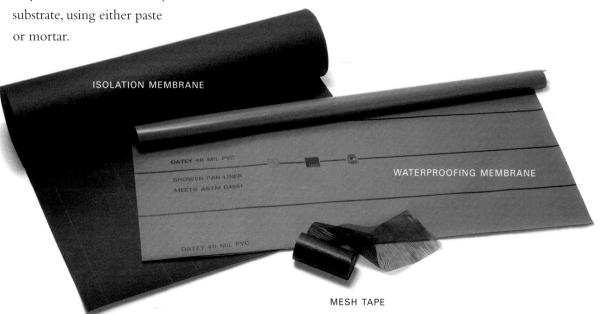

ISOLATION MEMBRANE

OATEY 40 MIL PVC
SHOWER PAN LINER
MEETS ASTM D4551

WATERPROOFING MEMBRANE

OATEY 40 MIL PVC

MESH TAPE

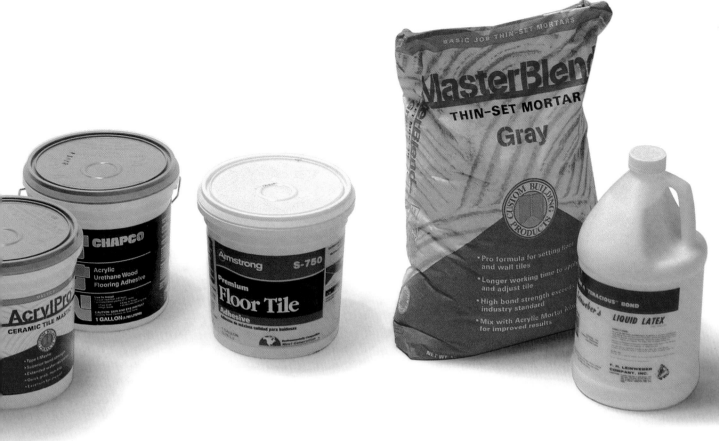

Adhesives

Consult with your tile dealer to find the best adhesive for your tile and substrate. Although circumstances may vary, in most cases the choice of adhesive is simple: Use thinset mortar for countertops and ceramic or stone floor tiles, and organic mastic for wall tiles and resilient or wood flooring.

Thinset mortar: To install ceramic or stone floor tile, latex-reinforced thinset mortar is usually the best choice. It comes in powdered form; you must mix it in small batches on the job and use it within about half an hour.

Latex reinforcement adds strength and a bit of flexibility to the thinset; without it, the thinset will crack easily. Some thinset comes with a powdered latex in the mix; just add water. A second variety requires you to add a liquid latex additive rather than water. The second type, with the liquid latex, is stronger.

Organic mastic: In a wet situation (such as a tub surround), you may choose to install wall tiles with thinset mortar; see pages 120 and 126–127. Organic mastic, which may be either oil- or latex-based, is easier

to use. It comes ready-mixed in a can or plastic tub; just spread it on the wall using a V-notched trowel, and set the tiles.

To install vinyl, cork, wood parquet, or laminate tile, use an organic mastic or glue specifically made for that tile.

Epoxy thinset: This expensive adhesive has three parts, which are mixed on the job. Use it in special situations where extra sticking strength is needed.

"Easy-to-use" products: Two products on the market advertise themselves as work-saving innovations. The first, ready-mixed floor tile adhesive, is a pre-mixed organic mastic that is said to save work and mess compared to thinset. Many homeowners have reported success with this product. Be aware, however, that it costs more and is not as strong as thinset mortar. The second is an "all in one" product, which acts as both adhesive and grout; the idea is that you can set the tiles and grout the joints in one fell swoop. Unfortunately, using this material will leave you with grout lines that are more porous and difficult to clean than standard grout.

TILING FLOORS

Floor tiles are available in a wide variety of sizes, colors, and prices to fit every need. Browse through the beginning of this chapter for just a sampling of possibilities. Unless your floor has serious structural problems, you can install any type of floor tile on it. In some cases, you may need to strengthen the floor a bit before laying heavy ceramic or stone tiles. See pages 54–55 to determine whether your floor is in need of a lift.

For almost all varieties of tile, a successful floor tile installation begins with a solid and flat substrate. (Resilient and wood flooring do not demand a firm substrate; go straight to page 80 for instructions on laying vinyl, wood parquet, or laminate tiles.) Pages 56–65 describe how to remove obstacles and prepare a surface that will be easy to tile. Then you'll learn how to lay out the job so tiles will look straight even when the room is out of square. The following instructions provide methods for cutting every type of ceramic or stone tile typically installed on a floor.

On pages 72–77, step-by-step instructions walk you through a ceramic tile floor installation. If you want to install stone or mosaic tiles, take a look at pages 78–79 as well.

Large synthetic stone tiles, with no base molding, help make this bathroom a gleaming modern space.

Light-colored marble in tiles and strips combined with small squares of darker colored marble creates a stately pattern.

Ceramic tiles of various colors and three different shapes form a regular pattern that gives the initial impression of patchwork.

Marble tiles cover the floor and countertop and serve as accents in the tub enclosure. An unobtrusive background of white wall tiles emphasizes the marble's natural beauty.

Though these ceramic tiles have a rustic, mottled appearance, straight, neat grout lines make the floor fit in with a modern kitchen.

The earthy look of saltillo tiles helps make this hallway an invitingly informal space. Exposed tile edges (rather than bullnose trim pieces) emphasize the roughness of the tile.

Black ceramic floor tiles make a simple yet dramatic contrast to an antique tub and gleaming glass wall tiles.

Nothing beats basic black and white for a classic formal look. In this hallway, polished marble tiles are laid with perfect symmetry.

Natural stone brings a bit of the outdoors into a room with large glass doors and windows. Here, large limestone tiles form a nearly seamless floor, a clean stage with limitless decorative possibilities.

These laminate tiles look just like stone, but are less expensive and easier to install. Copper-colored accent tiles, one-fourth the size of the field tiles, create an interlocking pattern.

On this kitchen floor, rectangular tiles of tumbled marble are laid in alternating directions, creating open squares filled with small accent tiles. The effect is similar to a basket weave pattern.

Handcrafted mosaic tile harks back to the floors of antiquity, yet creates an intimate atmosphere in a modern home. A section of mosaic tile requires painstaking work. Lay the tiles in a dry run on a piece of plywood before installing them.

MAKING SURE A FLOOR IS STRONG ENOUGH

Even very strong ceramic or stone tiles can crack if they are installed on a floor that is not firm. Many wood floors are already strong enough to support tile, and most can be made so by installing flooring backerboard. However, you may want to skip installing backerboard if it will cause the tiled floor to be more than ¾ inch above an adjacent floor. Also, a minority of floors have structural problems that backerboard cannot solve; in that case, repair the floor before proceeding.

Testing a Floor

A floor that is strong enough for tile will feel firm when a large adult jumps on it. If you feel any shaking, check out the structure. Find out how thick your subfloor is and how far apart the joists are. (If you need to remove existing flooring, do so before making any tests; see page 59.)

To measure the subfloor thickness, look for a hole in the floor—perhaps one drilled for a pipe—or drill a 1-inch hole in an inconspicuous spot, and stick a tape measure in the hole.

It's easy to find out how far apart your joists are spaced if the area below is an unfinished basement. If it's not, use a high-end stud finder that can detect joists even under wood flooring. Alternatively, drive a series of locator nails until you have found at least two joists. (Pull the nails up afterwards.)

The following specs satisfy normal residential requirements:

◆ If joists are spaced 16 inches apart, use a layer of plywood at least ¾ inch thick topped with ½-inch backerboard, or 1⅛ inches of plywood.

◆ If joists are spaced 24 inches apart, use a layer of plywood at least 1 inch thick (that is, two ½-inch sheets) topped with ½-inch backerboard, or 1½ inches of plywood.

◆ If you have an older home with angled 1-by plank subflooring, its strength depends on the type and condition of the planks. In very old homes, these may be rock-solid maple. If plank subflooring is firmly attached to joists, it is usually as strong as ¾-inch plywood.

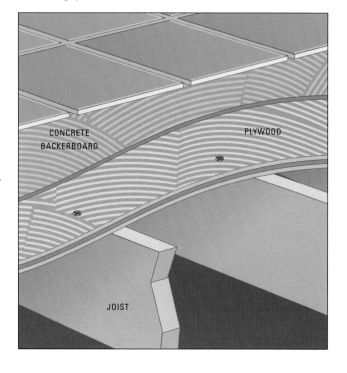

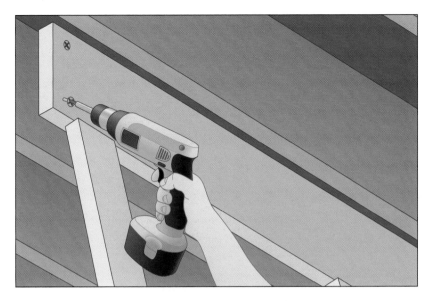

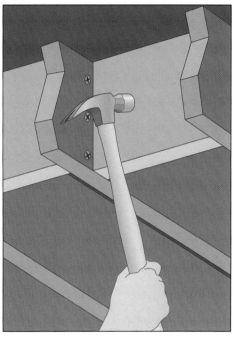

Strengthening a Floor

Often, a floor flexes not because it is too thin, but because the subflooring is inadequately attached. The solution may be to drive screws through the subfloor and into the joists. Use a stud finder to find the joists, and drive the screws using a drill equipped with a screwdriver bit. If you miss a joist, or if a screw does not grab firmly, remove the screw.

If a joist has sagged, however, driving screws may cause the floor to sag, and the joist itself may be weak. When the problem involves multiple joists, call in a carpenter for advice. To shore up a single joist, install a cleat (above, left). Cut the cleat out of 2-by material, making it as long as possible. Press it up against the bottom of the floor and hold it temporarily in place with 2-by-4 supports. Drive 3-inch wood screws every 8 inches or so to secure the cleat to the joist.

To strengthen an entire floor, install blocking (above, right). Cut pieces to fit tightly between the joists from 2-by stock that is the same width as the joists. Tap the blocking into place between the joists to form a fairly straight line. Drive screws at an angle to anchor the blocking to the joists.

ISOLATION MEMBRANE

If a floor is slightly springy, but adding backerboard would raise the top surface too high, check with your tile dealer or a professional tile setter to see whether an isolation membrane may be the right solution (see page 42). Such a membrane keeps tiles from cracking even when the surface it rests on is less than solid. Install the membrane as described on pages 64–65, laying it either in a special adhesive or in thinset mortar.

REMOVING OBSTACLES

It's very difficult to install floor tiles if anything is in the way. If at all possible, clear absolutely everything off the entire floor. In most cases, cutting tiles to fit around an obstruction is more time-consuming than removing the obstruction, tiling, and replacing the obstruction. And the resulting job will look neater.

Even an old, heavy radiator can be removed, or at least raised ½ inch so you can tile underneath it. To remove a steam radiator—that is, one with only one pipe leading into it—shut off the heat, loosen the nut, and pick up the radiator. If you've got a hot-water radiator (one with two pipes leading into it), be sure to drain the heating system before removing the radiator; consult with a heating specialist to learn how.

Removing a Toilet

Turn off the water supply at the toilet's shutoff valve. (If there is no shutoff valve, consult with a plumber; you may need to turn off water to the whole house.) Flush the toilet, and use a large sponge to remove as much water as possible from both the bowl and the tank. With a large pair of pliers or an adjustable wrench, unscrew and disconnect the riser tube, either at the toilet tank or at the valve.

Most toilets are held in place by only two nuts, screwed onto bolts that anchor the bowl to the floor. (Some older models may have bolts holding the tank to the wall.) Pry the decorative covers off the nuts, and use pliers or an adjustable wrench to unscrew each nut. If the nuts are too rusty to unscrew, cut through the bolts with a hacksaw.

Grasp the toilet bowl, and rock it back and forth until it comes loose from the wax ring underneath. Pick the entire toilet straight up, and carry it out. Some water may spill onto the floor. When reinstalling the toilet, you will need a new wax ring.

FLANGE EXTENDER

If tiling raises the floor more than ½ inch above the toilet flange, a wax ring may not be thick enough to reseal the toilet to the flange. Install two wax rings (one should have no plastic flange), or increase the flange's height with a toilet flange extender.

FLANGE EXTENDER

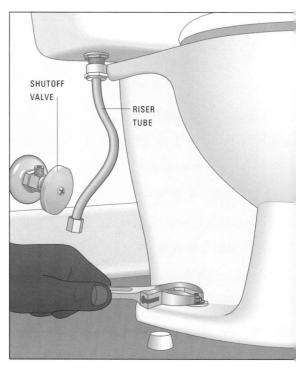

SHUTOFF VALVE

RISER TUBE

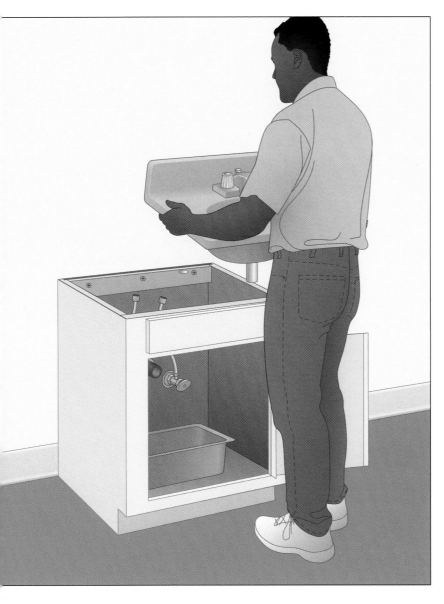

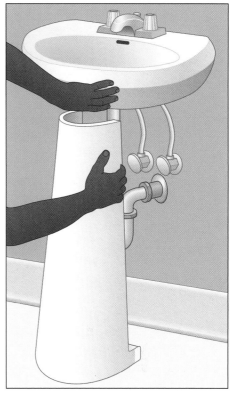

Removing a Sink Bottom

You may not have to remove the sink itself, but only the portion that rests on the floor. Details vary depending on the type of sink.

Vanity sink: To take out a vanity, you must remove the sink as well. Close the shutoff valves, and turn on the faucet to check that the hot and cold water are off. Disconnect the riser tubes from the shutoff valves. With a large wrench, loosen the nut that connects the tailpiece (the straight drain piece connected to the sink) to the drain trap below. If the sink is attached to the cabinet with adhesive, slice through the adhesive with a knife. Lift the sink out. Remove any screws or nails holding the cabinet in place, and remove it as well.

Removing a pedestal from a pedestal sink: Check to see if the pedestal is anchored to the floor with bolts; if so, remove the bolts. Gently lift up the sink, and slide the pedestal out. If the pedestal does not come out easily, you may need to remove the sink.

Wall-mounted sink: If a wall-mounted sink has legs reaching to the floor, you can probably remove them with little difficulty. You may need to twist the bottom portions of the legs to shorten them before removing.

Removing and Cutting Moldings

Many a homeowner has thought to save time by leaving moldings in place and cutting tiles to fit. Don't make this mistake. Systematically remove or cut all moldings, and plan your layout so that all tile edges will be covered once the moldings are back in place. If any of the existing molding looks worn, paint or replace it.

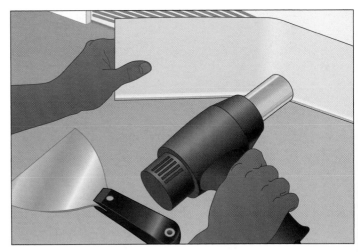

Vinyl cove base: Pry cove base off the wall using a stiff putty knife or a flat prybar. If the molding is stuck tight, use a heat gun to soften the adhesive as you pry. Install new cove base after tiling.

Wood baseboard: If the room has wood baseboard with a smaller bottom shoe piece, remove the shoe only. Using a utility knife, slice through the paint along the top of the shoe. Pry the shoe off using a flat prybar and a scrap of wood to protect the baseboard. If the shoe is in good shape, write numbers on the back of the pieces so you can easily replace them later.

If there is only a baseboard and no shoe, leave the baseboard in place and tile to within ½ inch of the molding; then install new base shoe. It's a good idea to paint pieces of base shoe or baseboard before installing them.

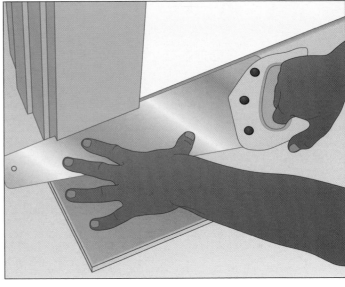

Door moldings: If you will be installing backerboard or plywood underlayment, save this step until the material is installed. Set a tile on the floor, and use it as a guide to cut the door casing so that you can slide tile under it. If you will be tiling the floor on both sides of the door, also cut the bottom of the doorjamb and the stop, using the same technique. To tile only to the middle of the jamb, leave the jamb alone and simply cut tiles to fit against it.

Preparing or Removing Old Flooring

If the floor has existing ceramic or vinyl flooring, you can choose to either install new tiles directly on top; remove the old flooring before tiling; or, in the case of vinyl, install backerboard directly on top (see page 61), and then install tiles. Whichever option you choose, make sure the floor is strong enough (see pages 54–55).

Resilient tiles or sheet flooring: Old resilient floorings include vinyl, linoleum, asphalt, and asbestos. If a single layer of non-cushioned resilient flooring is firmly attached, you can install ceramic or stone tile directly on top; for vinyl with a shiny surface, rough up the vinyl with a sanding block first.

Where there is more than one layer of resilient flooring, or where the flooring is cushioned, remove the flooring. If a stiff scraper does not do the job, use a flat prybar and a hammer. An iron can help soften the adhesive. Lay a cloth on top of the tiles, turn the iron to the highest setting, and iron the cloth, keeping the iron moving. After ten seconds or so, try prying up on the tile. If the adhesive is still not soft, repeat.

Ceramic tile: You can install new ceramic or stone tile directly on top of firmly attached ceramic or stone tile. If the old tile is glazed, rough up the surface using a belt sander, a tile stone, or a grinder, to ensure that the thinset will adhere. When the existing surface has deep grout lines, you can probably set large tiles on

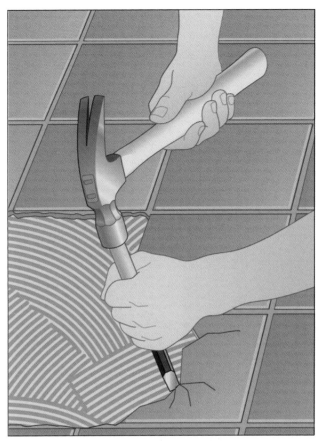

top with no problem, but small tiles may be uneven. Experiment first by laying down the new tiles without adhesive; if they form an uneven surface, fill the old grout lines with thinset, allowing it to dry before starting the tiling job. Removing ceramic tile can be difficult, especially if the tiles are set in an old-fashioned mortar bed. A cold chisel and hammer are usually the most efficient tools.

WARNING: WATCH OUT FOR ASBESTOS

Some old flooring contains asbestos, which can pose a serious health risk, especially if fragments are inhaled. If you have old flooring and don't know what it is made of, ask your local building department for ways to test for asbestos. Asbestos tiles are generally 9 inches square. If you do have asbestos flooring, some building codes require that it be removed, while others allow for it to be covered up. Never sand asbestos tile or remove it yourself; hire a company that specializes in asbestos removal.

PREPARING THE FLOOR

Consult pages 54–55 to make sure that the floor is strong enough for ceramic or stone tile—or that it will be, once you install backerboard. Remove any obstacles (see pages 56–59). Seal off doorways with plastic sheeting and duct tape to prevent dust from migrating throughout the house.

Patching a Damaged Floor

If an area of the subfloor is rotted or weak, adjust the depth of a circular saw blade so it cuts just through the subflooring without damaging underlying joists. Cut out a portion of the damaged area, determine where the joists are, and then widen the cut beyond the bad area so that it spans from joist to joist and forms a rectangle.

Cut two 2-by-6 nailers a little longer than the opening, and screw each to an outside joist. The top of each nailer should be the same height as the top of the joist it is attached to. Cut and install 2-by-6 blocking pieces to span between the joists, and attach them with angle-driven screws.

Install a plywood patch that has exactly the same thickness as the surrounding subfloor. If the floor's thickness is ⅞ inch or some other unusual dimension, place shims on top of the nailers and blocking pieces to bring the plywood patch up flush with the surrounding floor. Anchor the plywood patch with screws driven every 6 inches or so.

2 X 6 BLOCKING

2 X 6 NAILERS

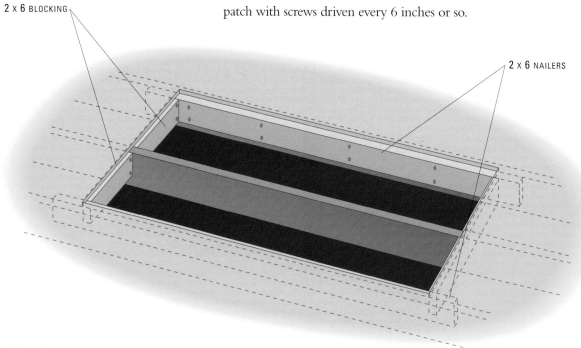

Installing Cement Backerboard

Purchase either mesh-reinforced or fibrous cement backerboard and special backerboard screws (see pages 40–41). With a chalk line, mark the floor to indicate the location of joists. Plan to install the sheets so none of the backerboard joints will be directly above joints in the subfloor. Stagger the joints in the backerboard so that there is no place where four corners meet. There should be a ⅛-inch gap between backerboard sheets, and a ¼-inch gap between the sheets and the wall or baseboard.

1 Score the line

Sweep the floor free of all debris, and lay down the sheet of backerboard to be cut. Measure for the cut, and subtract ¼ inch, since the cut end will be rough. Mark both the top and bottom of the cut, and hold a straightedge between the two marks. Or make only one mark, and hold a drywall square, as shown. Using a cement-backerboard knife, score a line.

2 Snap, score, and snap

Turn the sheet upside-down. Hold the board down on one side of the scored line and pull up on the other side until it snaps up. Pick the sheet up on its side, score along the same line on the back of the sheet, and snap it back again to free the cut piece. If the cut edge is very rough, smooth it a bit with a tile stone.

3 Attach the sheet

Sweep all debris from the floor. Mix thinset mortar (see page 73), and spread it on the floor using a ¼-inch square-notched trowel. Lay the sheet in the mortar carefully. Drive screws through the sheet into the joists every 6 inches, or as recommended by the manufacturer. Wherever the edge of a sheet is more than 2 inches away from a joist, drive screws along the edge every 4 inches or so.

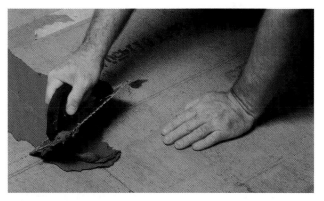

4 Tape the joints

Lay fiberglass mesh tape over all the joints. Using the flat edge of a trowel, spread a thin layer of thinset mortar over the tape. Feather it out on either side, and smooth away any high spots. After the thinset is hard, you're ready to tile.

I f a floor is seriously out of level, or if there are extensive depressions, you can straighten out the situation with self-leveling compound. Mix the compound with water, then simply pour it onto the area that needs leveling; little or no troweling is needed. Some products dry in an hour or two. Self-leveling compound can be poured to a depth of no more than 1 inch; if you need additional thickness, allow the first batch to set, then repeat the process.

Preparing a Concrete Surface

If a concrete floor is still strong after years of use, it is probably sturdy enough to support tiles. In the case of a floor that is cracked so that one side of the crack is higher than the other, install an isolation membrane (see pages 64–65).

Drag a long, straight board across the floor, and look for high or low spots. With a pencil or crayon, mark all the high spots, as well as any depressions deeper than ¼ inch.

Leveling high spots: Knock down a small high spot using a cold chisel and hammer. For larger areas, use a grinder.

Patching a crack: A trowel-applied membrane will isolate small cracks less than ¼ inch wide. For a wider crack, chisel out any loose particles from inside the crack and fill it with patching concrete.

Handling different surface materials or isolation joints: If a concrete floor abuts a wood floor, the two surfaces will move separately over the years. On a concrete surface, you may find an isolation joint (a gap of ¼ inch or more, filled with caulk or fibrous material), which essentially divides the surface into independent slabs. In either circumstance, apply a 2-foot-wide strip of professional-quality isolation membrane over the joint (see page 42).

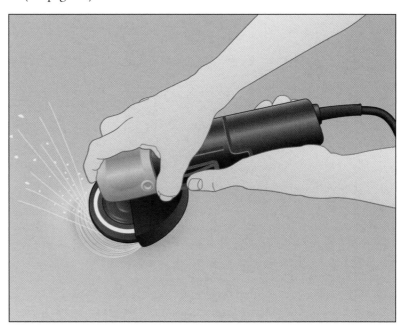

WET CONCRETE

Filling a depression or a hole: Use a cold hammer and chisel to chip away any loose concrete in a dip or a hole. Brush latex concrete bonding agent over the area, and let it dry. Fill in the depression with latex-reinforced concrete patch. If the area is wider than 2 feet, use a straight board to level the patch roughly. Smooth the patch with the flat side of a trowel and allow it to dry.

CHOOSING A THRESHOLD

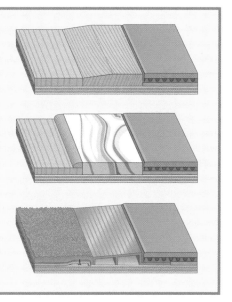

In situations where the tiled floor will be higher than an adjacent wood or tile floor, plan to step down gracefully with a beveled threshold. If a standard hardwood threshold (top) does not slope down far enough to meet the adjacent floor, use a belt sander to increase the angle. If you cannot find a marble threshold in the right shape, consider using a non-beveled piece and adding a small piece of hardwood trim along the edge (middle). For tiles that will abut a carpeted floor, install a metal carpet strip on top of the joint (see page 92), or butt perfectly cut tiles up against a carpet strip and apply grout to the joint (bottom).

Installing Membranes

In most cases, ceramic or stone tile can be installed directly on top of a backerboard or plywood underlayment. However, if the floor tends to flex, consider installing an isolation membrane. And if the floor will get wet for prolonged periods, it's a good idea to install a waterproofing membrane. See page 42 for information on choosing both types of membranes.

Securing a paper-backed membrane: Sweep and mop the floor to clear away even the smallest bits of debris. Roll the membrane out, and use a utility knife and a straightedge to cut pieces to fit. Follow the manufacturer's directions as to how much side-by-side pieces should overlap. After cutting each piece, roll up both ends, so the piece looks like a scroll. Note the order and direction in which each piece will be laid.

Follow the manufacturer's directions on how to spread the adhesive paste. Most recommend a thick-napped paint roller. Spread adhesive for one piece of membrane at a time, and wait for the adhesive to dry so that it is tacky.

The membrane has a wax-paper backing that will not stick to the adhesive. With the backing still attached, place a piece of membrane on the adhesive, unroll both ends, and position it precisely. Taking care that the piece does not go out of alignment, roll up half of the membrane. Cut through the paper backing, and start peeling the paper off, slowly rolling the exposed membrane onto the adhesive as you work. The membrane will stick firmly as soon as it meets the adhesive. Once that half of the membrane has been rolled out, smooth any wrinkles with the flat edge of a trowel. Repeat the process for the other half of the piece.

After installing all the membrane pieces, you can start troweling on thinset and setting tiles.

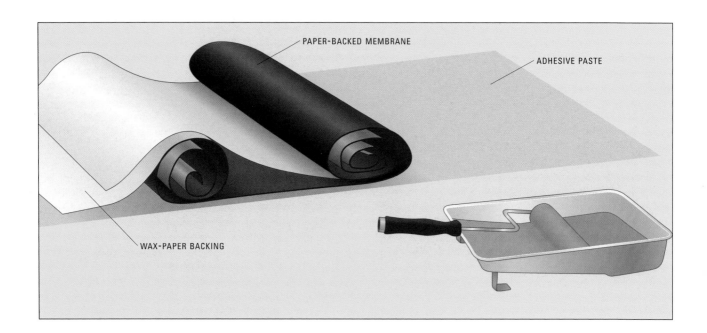

PAPER-BACKED MEMBRANE

ADHESIVE PASTE

WAX-PAPER BACKING

Embedding a membrane in thinset:
Another method of applying a membrane is simpler, but more time-consuming. Spread thinset mortar—the same material that you will use to set the tiles—onto the floor using a notched trowel. Lay the pieces of membrane in the thinset, and embed them using a sheet-flooring roller. After the thinset has set, trowel on another layer of thinset in which to set the tiles.

EXPANSION JOINTS

Ceramic and stone tiles expand and contract with changes of temperature. This movement is so slight that it rarely has an impact on residential floors, which tend to be smaller than commercial installations. If, however, a floor extends further than 30 feet in any direction, be safe and install an expansion joint. The simplest way is to fill one grout line with silicone caulk instead of grout. Allow the caulk to dry before you fill all the other lines with grout. The caulked line will be flexible, so that tiles can move

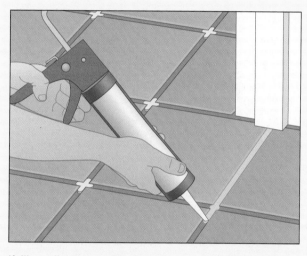

If tiling adjoining rooms results in more than 30 linear feet of tile, fill the grout line at the doorway with caulk instead of grout to create an expansion joint. Use silicone caulk that matches the color of the grout, and allow it to dry completely before grouting.

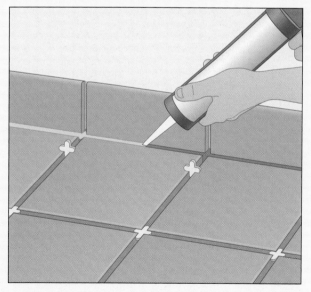

A wall moves differently than the floor below it. Caulk the joint rather than grouting.

without cracking. If you're installing tile on a very large floor, buy contractor-style expansion joints instead, and install them at regular intervals.

Water pipes expand and contract quite a bit. When cutting tiles to go around a water pipe, always allow for a gap at least $\frac{1}{8}$ inch wide between the tile and the pipe. Fill the gap with silicone caulk or leave it bare, but don't fill the gap with grout.

LAYING OUT A FLOOR

Once you're sure the floor is strong enough and smooth enough for tile, it's time to think through the layout. There are three basic considerations:

♦ Avoid ending up with narrow tile slivers along one or more walls. There's one exception: If you are sure that one edge of the floor will always be hidden, say, by furniture, then you may choose to install slivers there in order to have wide pieces along the opposite wall.

♦ If you can do so without ending up with slivers, center the tiles in a room so that the cut tiles on opposite edges are the same size. This is particularly important if the room is small.

♦ If a room is out of square, adjust the layout to hide this imperfection as much as possible. Sometimes you can decide which edge of the floor will have tiles that slowly increase in width along its length; if so, choose the edge along the least visible wall. Make the tiles along this edge as wide as possible, since narrower tiles will make the imperfection more obvious.

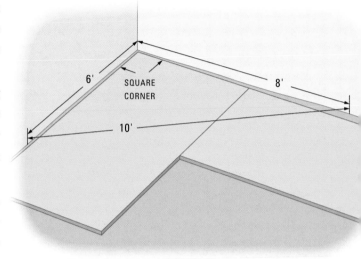

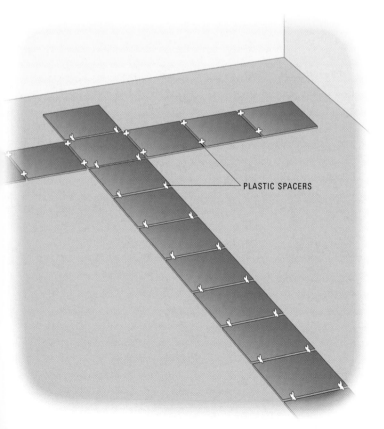

PLASTIC SPACERS

Checking if a Room is Square

Lay full sheets of plywood or drywall (which have perfectly square corners) on the floor with the edges 1 inch away from both walls. Measure to see if either wall goes out of square along its length. Also check for waves in the walls.

Alternatively, use the "3-4-5" method. Mark one wall precisely 3 feet from a corner, and the other wall 4 feet from the corner. If the distance between these two marks is exactly 5 feet, then the corner is square. If the room is large enough, use multiples of 3, 4, and 5, such as 6, 8, and 10 (as shown above) or 9, 12, and 15.

Laying Tiles in a Dry Run

It's easy to make a mistake when figuring a layout mathematically. Take no chances: lay complete rows of full-sized tiles, with spacers, on the floor in at least two directions (as shown at left). This will tell you the exact size of the cut tiles along the edges. Chances are, you'll make an adjustment or two once you see the layout. Use this dry run to mark the floor for working lines (see page 69).

Drawing Out-of-Square and Complicated Areas

If a room has more than four corners or is more than 1 inch out of square, or if multiple adjacent rooms are involved, make a drawing to help you visualize the job. Lay ten tiles in a dry run with plastic spacers, measure the distance the tiles cover, and add the thickness of one grout line. Divide by 10, and you've got an accurate per-tile length.

Make a drawing on graph paper. Decide on a scale that is easy to use—say, one tile (including the adjoining grout line) per graph square, or one tile per four squares. Be sure to draw the room accurately; measure so you can show any out-of-square walls precisely. Make several photocopies of this room drawing, so you can experiment with different tile layouts.

If a layout is complicated—particularly if you are tiling adjacent rooms—you may need to make compromises (as shown below). After you've made one drawing, you may decide to move all the tiles over an inch or two, to avoid or hide slivers, or to minimize the visual impact of an out-of-square wall.

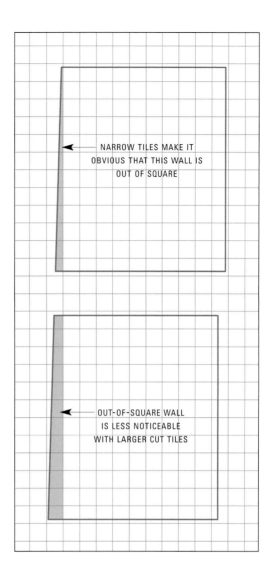

NARROW TILES MAKE IT OBVIOUS THAT THIS WALL IS OUT OF SQUARE

OUT-OF-SQUARE WALL IS LESS NOTICEABLE WITH LARGER CUT TILES

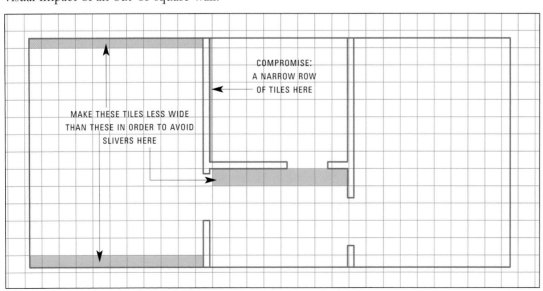

COMPROMISE: A NARROW ROW OF TILES HERE

MAKE THESE TILES LESS WIDE THAN THESE IN ORDER TO AVOID SLIVERS HERE

Making a Jury Stick

If a room is large or the layout is complicated, a jury stick (also called a layout stick) can simplify the planning process. To make a jury stick, find or cut a narrow board, such as a strip of plywood or a piece of 1-by-2 lumber, about 8 feet long. Set the board on the floor next to some tiles laid with spacers in a dry run, positioning the end in the center of a grout line. Mark the board at the center of each grout line. Make sure the board remains stable while you mark it.

Use a jury stick as a kind of instant dry run. When laid on the floor, it tells you how many tiles will fit in a given area, as well as how wide the cut pieces will be.

LAYOUT FOR DIAGONAL TILES

To mark for tiles that will be laid diagonally in a room, snap two perpendicular chalk lines that meet in the exact center of the room. Use a full sheet of plywood or the "3-4-5" method (see page 66) to make sure the lines are exactly perpendicular. Then mark points along all four lines that are equally distant from the center. Take care to be precise with these measurements.

Now snap chalk lines that connect the marks you have just made; this will result in a square that is tilted at a 45-degree angle to the room. Use the sides of this square as working lines for laying out the room.

Lay tiles in a dry run. You may need to shift the tiles an inch or so in order to avoid having very small cut triangular tiles at the edges.

Marking the Working Lines

Once you've settled on a layout, it's time to draw the working lines that you'll use as guides for the first tiles you lay. First, decide where you want to start tiling, so you will never have to step on recently laid tiles. In some cases, it makes sense to start in the middle of the room; in other cases, it's best to start a few feet from a wall. If a room has only one door, start at the far end of the room and work toward the door. If you want to install the cut tiles at the same time as the full tiles, make sure you never have to reach across more than 3 feet of tiles in order to lay a cut tile.

To mark a working line, make a V-shaped mark at either end, with the tip of the V representing the exact end of the line. Have a helper hold one end of a chalk line centered on one mark. Or tack a nail at the mark, and hook the chalk line to it. Pull out the line and center it over the other mark. Then pull the line taut, pick it straight up several inches, and let go. If the resulting line is not clear, snap the chalk line again. If it is still not clear, roll up the line to recoat it with chalk, and try again. Snap two perpendicular lines (as shown above).

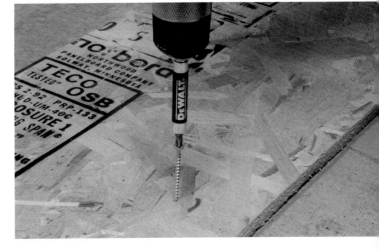

Using a Batten

To ensure that your first line of tiles will be straight, tack down a long, straight board known as a batten. The factory edge of a ¾-inch sheet of plywood makes an ideal batten, because it is perfectly straight and thick enough that tiles cannot slide over it. Position the batten next to a working line, and drive several screws to hold it firmly to the floor. Butt the first row of tiles up to it. Once the mortar starts to harden, remove the batten. You may be able to use it again elsewhere.

CUTTING FENCE

Cutting Floor Tiles

The cutting techniques described here apply to ceramic, quarry, and most porcelain tiles. Stone, terra-cotta, cement-body, and some porcelain tiles should be cut with a wet saw only. (To determine which technique to use for specific porcelain tiles, consult your dealer.) For instructions on cutting wall tiles, see page 113.

Using a snap cutter: Mark a cut line on the tile with a pencil or a felt-tipped marker. Position the tile firmly against the snap cutter's front guide so the cut will be square. Lift up the handle, and push or pull it to score a line all the way across the tile. It's best to score a single, continuous line, but if you score an incomplete line, go over it again. Allow the wings of the cutter to rest on either side of the scored line, and push down on the handle; the tile will snap in two. Brush away all debris from the base of the cutter before making the next cut.

For a series of cuts that are the same size, position the first tile for a cut and clamp the cutting fence against it. To cut the next tile, hold it against the fence.

Using a nibbling tool: It may seem unlikely that this simple tool can cut curves and notches in hard floor tiles, but all it takes is practice and patience. Nibbled cuts often will not be crisp and precise, but they are accurate enough for most purposes.

To make a cut that runs in two directions, first score the lines using a snap cutter. Then start taking small bites out of the cut-out area. The key is to nibble slowly, taking lots of tiny bites; if you take a big bite, you'll probably shatter the tile. Work your way slowly toward the corner of the cut. When you reach the scored lines, you can nibble more accurately.

It is usually not possible to cut off less than ½ inch from a floor tile using a snap cutter. To remove a slender slice from a tile, score the line with the snap cutter, then use a nibbling tool to break off the waste side of the cut, piece by piece.

Cutting with a wet saw: A tile-cutting wet saw makes the cleanest cuts in floor tiles. A rented saw typically has a pump that squirts water through a tube onto a rotating diamond blade. The pump must be submerged in water at all times; if the blade cuts even for a few seconds while it is dry, it can become dull. An inexpensive wet saw (see page 37) typically has its blade partly submerged in water, so there is no need for a pump.

If the saw is equipped with a splash guard, you can use it indoors as long as you don't mind some scattered spray, but working outside will guarantee a dry room. Set the saw on a work table or two stable saw horses. For a saw with a pump, fill the pan with water, set the pump in the water, and test to make sure there is a continuous stream directed at the blade while it is on. For other saws, just make sure the water supply is filled.

To make a straight cut, slide the tray all the way back toward you and position the tile, pressing it firmly against the guide. Turn on the saw, and slide the tile forward. Hold the tile firmly in place on the tray at all times, but press gently against the blade as you cut through the tile.

ANGLED CUTTING FENCE

For a 45-degree cut, use a special angled cutting fence. Protractor-type fences are available if you need to make cuts at angles other than 45 or 90 degrees.

NOTCH CUTS

To cut out a notch, first use a snap cutter to score the frontmost cut line. Hold the tile at a steep angle, so that the saw blade will cut deeper on the back side. Make a series of cuts, about ¼ inch apart, that end at the cut line. Finish by using a nibbling tool to clean up the edge.

INSTALLING A PATTERNED FLOOR

If a flooring pattern uses a defined ensemble of tiles, so that its size cannot be adjusted, set it in a dry run in the center of the room to see if you will end up with unattractive slivers of tile at the room's edges. If so, consider moving the pattern an inch or two out of center.

Other patterns can be adjusted for size by cutting some of the tiles. In that case, lay the floor out for an attractive overall fit of the surrounding tiles, and then design the patterned section.

In either case, draw precise working lines for the patterned section, and install it first. Then install the surrounding tiles.

LAYING A CERAMIC TILE FLOOR

Once mortar starts to harden—something that can happen quickly, depending on weather conditions—adjusting the position of a tile is all but impossible. Before you mix the mortar, review pages 54–71 to make sure all your ducks are in a row. See that the floor is strong and the surface is smooth and level. Remove all obstacles and, if needed, the base molding. Plan ahead for any thresholds. Set tiles in a dry run and draw the layout on the floor.

The instructions for this project apply to any ceramic tile, including porcelain pavers, quarry tile, cement-body tile, and terra-cotta tile. Additional directions for installing stone tiles and mosaics are given on pages 78–79. To install saltillos or other irregularly shaped tiles, see pages 166–169.

The Order of Work

If a room is small and uncomplicated, set all the tiles in one day. For a larger job, you may choose to install all the full-sized tiles one day, then install the cut tiles a day or two later, after the full-sized tiles have set enough so that you can walk on them. If you are renting a wet saw for the cuts, this ensures that you will not have to pay for an extra day's rental.

Plan the tiling sequence so that you will never need to step on a tile that you have just laid; doing so could move it out of alignment. If you expect to tile the room in one day, make sure that you will never have to lean over more than 3 feet of just-installed tiles in order to measure and place a cut tile.

Applying Mortar

For most applications, use gray thinset mortar with a liquid latex additive (see page 43). If the tile is at all translucent (as with glass tile or marble), use white thinset mortar. A small amount of mortar can be mixed by hand with a margin trowel, but you'll save trouble and produce a more reliable mix if you use a mixing paddle and a rented ½-inch drill. Mix only as much thinset as you can use within 30 minutes or so (allot less time if the weather is dry and warm). The dry mix and the liquid should be at room temperature before you start.

1 Mix the mortar

Pour a few inches of latex into the bucket, then add the powdered thinset. Set the paddle down into the bucket. Hold the bucket firmly with your feet to keep it from spinning as you mix. Operate the drill in short bursts at first—liquid may spray out of the bucket if you hold the trigger too long. Keep mixing until all lumps are gone.

2 Test and prepare the mortar

The thickness of the mortar is critical. It should be wet enough to pour, and just thick enough to stick to a trowel for a second or two when held upside-down. Add liquid or powder as needed. Wait 10 minutes, then mix the mortar briefly again.

3 Spread the mortar

Pour some thinset mortar onto the floor, or scoop it out with a notched trowel. Use a trowel with notches sized for your type of tile (see page 38). With the trowel held fairly flat, spread the mortar over an area about 4 feet square, taking care not to cover any working lines.

4 Comb with a notched trowel

Turn the trowel around so the notches are down. For consistent mortar thickness, hold the trowel and maintain the same angle at all times as you comb. Allow the teeth of the trowel to scrape the subfloor gently, and use long, sweeping strokes wherever possible. Comb away all globs of mortar. Once the mortar starts to harden, don't try adding liquid; throw the mortar out.

Setting Tiles

For a professional-looking job, tiles should be set in straight lines with grout lines of consistent width, and the surface of the tiles should form a smooth plane. Check for both these things every 10 minutes or so; adjusting tiles after that may weaken the thinset bond. Stretch a string line next to a row of tiles, or butt a very straight board gently against the tiles; the factory edge of a piece of plywood works well. Also check that the tiles form a level surface.

1 Set the tiles with spacers

Set each tile fairly precisely, so you don't have to slide it more than an inch or so. Align the first tile with two working lines, then set several more tiles, inserting spacers at every corner. Don't press down on any tile.

2 Tap with a beater board

Set a beater board over two or more tiles, and tap. This helps ensure that the tile bottom is set firmly in the mortar and it also aligns the top surface of one tile with its neighbor. Periodically check to see that the tiles form a continuous, level plane.

3 Check adhesion

About every 10 minutes, pick up a tile that you've just set, and look at the back. Mortar should adhere to the entire surface. If you find only partial adhesion, perhaps the mortar is too dry; scrape it off the floor and throw it out. Or perhaps the mortar was not combed to a flat surface; recomb it.

4 Remove excess mortar

Remove any excess mortar as you go; it will be much harder to remove when it dries. A carpenter's pencil works well for removing mortar between tiles. Or use spacers, as shown. Keep the job site as clean as possible.

To adjust a tile slightly, place your hand on top, fingers splayed out. Press gently as you slide the tile. If you feel resistance followed by a sudden movement, the mortar has probably begun to set. Pick up the tile and attempt to recomb the mortar below. If the mortar has started to harden, scrape the tile and the floor below it clean of mortar, and start over.

Run the edge of a straight board along the tile surface to test that they form a level surface. If a tile is too high, try pressing down on all four corners. If a tile is too low, remove it, apply additional mortar, and reset it.

Cutting Tiles

See pages 70–71 for cutting techniques. If a cut will be covered with molding, it doesn't need to be perfect. Just make sure the tile edge will not show after the molding is installed, and leave a gap of at least ⅛ inch between the tile and the wall. If the cut edge will show, take the time to cut precisely.

BACK-BUTTER EDGE TILES

If a cut tile is narrower than your notched trowel, apply mortar to the back of the tile rather than to the floor. "Back-butter" with care. Apply enough mortar so the cut tile is as high as the adjacent one, but not so much that mortar oozes out of the joint.

1 Mark for the cut

To mark for a straight cut, place a spacer against the wall that is as thick as the grout line. Place the tile to be cut on top of the adjacent whole tile, aligning the two precisely. Set another tile on top of it, and slide the top tile against the spacer. Use the top tile to draw the cut line.

2 Mark for the second cut

At an inside corner, first mark and cut the tile to fit in one direction, then mark the second cut.

Applying Grout

Once all the tiles are set, allow the mortar to set for at least 12 hours before walking on the floor. If the weather is humid, or if any of the exposed mortar is not completely dry, wait another day. The mortar will become lighter in color as it dries.

Use a thin screwdriver to pry all the spacers out. Take care not to nick the tile as you work. (Some installers leave spacers in place if they are sunk at least ¼ inch below the surface of the tile, but this increases the likelihood that grout will crack.) Wherever mortar is less than ¼ inch below the surface of the tile, dig it out with the screwdriver. Wipe away all mortar on the surface of the tile using a wet rag or a scrubber.

Unless the grout joints are less than ⅛ inch wide, use a sanded grout. If the grout is fortified with a powdered latex, add water. If the grout does not contain powdered latex, add liquid latex, even if the directions say you can use water.

1 Mix the grout

Pour a small amount of grout powder into a clean bucket. Slowly add liquid latex or water, mixing with a trowel as you go, until the grout is about the thickness of toothpaste and free of lumps. Wait for 10 minutes, then mix again. Add a little more liquid if necessary.

2 Push grout into place

Using a laminated grout float, scoop some grout onto the floor. Holding the float nearly flat, push the grout into the grout lines using sweeping back-and-forth strokes. At every point on the floor, be sure to push the grout with strokes running in two or more directions.

3 Wipe away the excess

Tip the float up and use it like a squeegee to clear away most of the grout from the surface of the tiles. Move the float across the tiles diagonally, so the edge of the float does not dig into any grout lines. Aim to remove at least three-quarters of the surface grout, but don't worry if you miss a few spots.

Wiping and Jointing

Once the grout is firmly embedded and most of the excess has been wiped away, it's time to remove the rest of the excess grout and to make consistent grout lines, a process called jointing. Don't take this process lightly; it's more than "just cleaning." A tile job that has been wiped carelessly will look unprofessional.

Have a bucket of clean water on hand, so you can continually rinse the sponge. Once the water starts to get murky, change the water.

As you work, take care not to step or kneel in the grout lines. Work systematically, one section at a time. If you were able to squeegee nearly all the surface grout away using a float (step 3, opposite), move to step 1. Otherwise, wet a large towel, and squeeze some of the water out of it so it is wet but not dripping. Lay it on top of the tiles—do not push it in—and drag it across the tiles, to remove most of the excess grout. Turn the towel over or rinse it out before dragging it again.

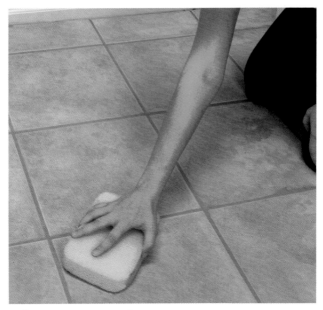

1 Wipe with a sponge
Dip a large sponge in clean water and squeeze some of the water out, so the sponge is wet but not dripping. Run the sponge across the tile surface gently to wipe grout from the tile surfaces, but do not dig into the grout lines. Repeat this process at least once.

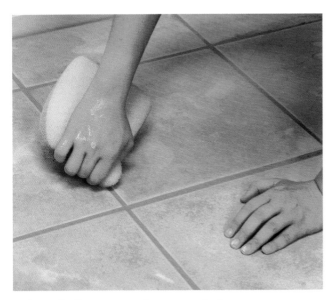

2 Make consistent joints
Floor grout should be just slightly below the tile surface; deeper grout will be hard to keep clean. Moisten a sponge with clean water and wring it out so it is just damp. Run it along each grout line, working first in one direction, then in the other. You may find it easier to work if you ball up a corner of the sponge.

3 Buff away the haze
Allow the grout to dry; it will become lighter in color. Using a dry, lint-free rag, buff the surface of the tiles until they shine. If any holes appear in the grout lines, fill them with grout.

LAYING A STONE TILE FLOOR

Either polished or rough stone tile can usually be installed wherever ceramic tile is used. In general, employ the same techniques as those shown on pages 54–79. However, you'll probably have to make all the cuts with a wet saw rather than a snap cutter or nippers. Light-colored marble, travertine, and other natural stones are somewhat translucent; gray thinset mortar can show through enough to muddy their appearance. Use white thinset instead. Some types of stone soak up stains readily, so grout of a contrasting color may stain the stone as you apply it. Sealing the tile before installing may keep it from staining; consult with your tile dealer.

Polished Stone

Typically, formal-looking polished stone (above) is installed with thin grout lines. Use $1/16$-inch spacers and unsanded grout. Because the tiles are placed so close together, even the slightest discrepancy in height would be noticeable. Start with a substrate that is absolutely smooth. Some stone tiles are slightly warped; before applying mortar, lay tiles next to each other to test for imperfections. Take extra care while combing the mortar to achieve a very even surface. When you set the tiles, check constantly for changes in level and use a beater board to make corrections.

Informal Stone

Tumbled marble and other porous stones (left) usually are installed with wide grout lines, and the finished floor is not expected to be perfectly smooth. As a result, installation is much less nerve-wracking than for polished stone.

It can be difficult to clean grout from porous stone, however. It may be necessary to seal the tiles before applying grout; check with your tile dealer. When you apply the grout, wipe the tiles with a clean, wet sponge early and often.

LAYING A MOSAIC TILE FLOOR

When installing large tiles, it's usually fine if 20 percent or so of the tile is not embedded in the mortar. But with small mosaic tiles, every square inch must nestle firmly in the mortar, or else one of the individual tiles may come loose. The problem is compounded by the fact that many mosaics have a paper or mesh backing that is hard for mortar to stick to. To make sure that all the tiles stick, a sheet of mosaics must be pressed very firmly into the mortar. Typically, this causes mortar to ooze up through the many grout lines, making installing mosaics a messy operation.

If the individual tiles are large enough, you can cut mosaics using a snap cutter. Usually, however, a nibbling tool is easier. To make a precise cut in a small tile, first score the line with a snap cutter, then cut with a nibbling tool. To remove entire mosaic tiles from a sheet, simply use a knife.

To ensure firm adhesion, spend a little more for epoxy thinset. If you work carefully, however, standard thinset mortar, mixed with liquid latex, should do the job.

In either case, mix the mortar a little wetter than you would for regular tiles—it should be barely firm enough so that the ridges made by a notched trowel hold their shape. Mix small amounts, because you will work slowly.

As you lay the sheets in mortar, check often to make sure all the tiles are sticking. Tap the tiles firmly into the mortar using a beater board. When mortar oozes up between the tiles, wipe it off with a damp—not wet—sponge; getting the remaining mortar wet could weaken it. Wiping the mortar away to a depth of at least $\frac{1}{4}$ inch is a tedious but necessary job.

When you apply the grout, you won't be able to tool every line as you would with larger tiles. Keep wiping the surface lightly (below), over and over again, until the grout lines are consistent in depth.

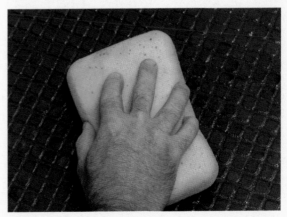

INSTALLING RESILIENT TILES

In most respects, installing vinyl composition or solid vinyl tiles is quite a bit easier than installing ceramic or stone tile. The substrate does not have to be firm, because these tiles are flexible. Figuring the layout is easy, since most resilient tiles are 12 inches square, with no grout lines. No special cutting tools are needed; a utility knife works well, though renting a vinyl tile cutter will save time. The job is usually done in a day, and you can walk on the floor right after you install it.

Preparing the Surface

A resilient floor does have one stringent requirement, however: the substrate must be extremely smooth. Thin tiles with embossed patterns (which are usually self-stick) will reflect even tiny imperfections in the floor below. Vinyl composition tiles are thicker, but only slightly more forgiving.

Remove all obstructions from the floor. Pry off the existing base molding, and plan to replace it later, so all tile edges will be covered (see pages 56–59).

Tiling over resilient flooring: If the floor has existing resilient flooring in good shape, glue down any loose pieces, and carefully fill and sand any holes. To install resilient tile over an existing floor with an embossed surface, first smooth out the surface by troweling on, and then sanding, a special embossing leveler.

Installing plywood underlayment: If the floor is not smooth, cover it with plywood underlayment, available in 4-foot square sheets with stamped cross marks. Cut the plywood with a circular saw. When you install it, make sure that the factory edges butt against each other, positioning any cut edges at the edges of the room. Offset the corners, so that four pieces never come together in one place. To attach the plywood, you can either drive a screw at every other cross mark, or drive a staple at every cross mark using a rented pneumatic subflooring stapler. Whichever method you use, make sure that all fastener heads are sunk below the plywood surface.

Using the flat edge of a trowel, fill all the holes—including the lines between the sheets and the screw or staple holes—with ready-mixed flooring patch (as shown above). Allow the patch to dry, then sand the entire floor smooth.

Tiling over concrete: Before installing resilient tiles on a concrete surface, use a grinder to take down any high spots, and fill holes with floor patch. Clean an old floor with concrete cleaner to make sure that the adhesive will bond to it.

Planning the Layout

See pages 66–69 for instructions on laying out a floor. Often, two or more colors of vinyl composition tile are installed in a pattern. Create a pattern using graph paper, or lay the tiles in a dry run on the floor to see how they look. All the tiles on a floor should be made by the same manufacturer to ensure they will be precisely the same size. If you are installing over an existing tile floor, offset the new tiles so that the edges are at least 2 inches away from the edges of the old tiles.

When deciding where to start installing the tiles, keep in mind that you cannot step on the adhesive after it has been applied with the trowel; you can, however, step on tiles as soon as they are laid. Either start in the middle of the floor and install the adhesive and tiles in two sections, or trowel adhesive over the entire floor and then start laying tiles near the entry door and working inward.

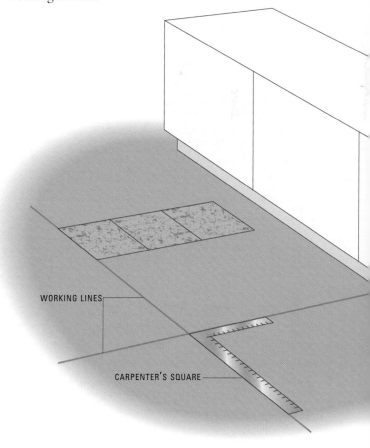

WORKING LINES

CARPENTER'S SQUARE

Setting the Tiles

Installing resilient tiles is not difficult, but you must work systematically. Check the label on the adhesive to make sure your trowel has notches of the correct dimensions—usually, $5/32$ by $1/16$. Spread the adhesive carefully, aiming for even coverage with no blobs. Install tiles in the order shown at right, starting at the intersection of the two working lines and fanning outward. As you set each tile, bend over and squint to see that its corners align precisely with the corners of adjacent tiles. Have a rag and some adhesive remover or paint thinner ready to remove excess adhesive.

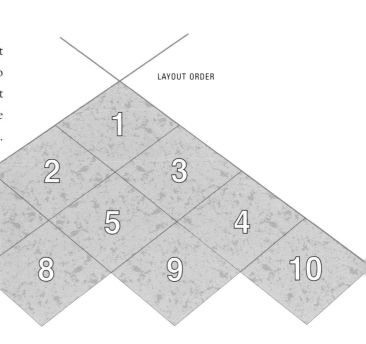

LAYOUT ORDER

1 Spread the adhesive

Tilt the bucket of adhesive and shake a dollop onto the floor. Holding the trowel at about a 45-degree angle to the floor, spread the adhesive. Use long, sweeping strokes that overlap by an inch or so. Trowel away any excess adhesive immediately. Don't try to retrowel it a few minutes later, because the adhesive will have started to harden. It's fine to cover the working lines with adhesive; you'll be able to see them again when the adhesive hardens.

2 Lay the first tile

After half an hour or so, depending on the temperature and humidity, the adhesive will become translucent and tacky rather than wet. You now have 8 hours or so to lay the tiles. Gently position the first tile at the intersection of the working lines; don't push down on it. Examine the position of this first one very carefully, to see that it follows the lines in both directions.

3 Lay more tiles

Lay the next two tiles in place, and check to see that they are following the working lines. If they are going off the lines, you should be able to adjust their position slightly. After three or four more tiles have been installed, adjustments will be impossible. Continue laying tiles, following the order shown in the illustration on the opposite page. Whenever you install a tile that butts against only one other tile, feel the corners to make sure that they line up precisely.

4 Clean away excess adhesive

Occasionally, adhesive will squeeze up between two tiles. Immediately use a rag soaked with adhesive remover or paint thinner to wipe this away.

5 Walk it down

From time to time, stand up and walk all over the floor, pressing straight down with your foot to firmly embed each tile in the adhesive. Afterwards, clean off any adhesive that squeezes up.

INSTALLING SELF-STICK TILES

The selling point for these tiles is that they have a sticky back, so they can be simply applied to a dry floor. However, some pros distrust the adhesive on the back of the tiles, and spread vinyl adhesive just as they would for non-stick tiles.

Lay out in the same way as for vinyl composition tile. Peel off each tile's paper backing, and install the tiles along the working lines. Cut any edge tiles with the backing still in place; these tiles are so thin that they can be cut clean through with one pass of a utility knife.

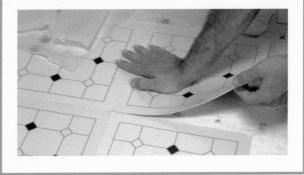

Cutting Vinyl Tiles

Once all the full tiles have been installed, lay some plywood on the floor to use as a cutting surface. If you have lots of cutting to do, you could rent a vinyl tile cutter. However, a utility knife should work just as well.

1 Mark for a straight cut
To measure for a straight cut, place a ¼-inch spacer against the wall. Turn the tile upside-down, facing in the correct direction, and hold it over its future location, pressed against the spacer. Mark both sides for the cut. Keep the tile from touching the adhesive while you are measuring.

2 Score with a knife
Hold a straightedge between the two marks. (A full tile makes a convenient straightedge. Mark it with an X so you will not install it on the floor by mistake.) With a utility knife, score a single line along the straightedge.

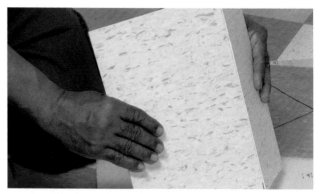

3 Snap the tile
Pick the tile up, hold both sides firmly, and bend the tile until it snaps.

CUTTING FOR AN OUTSIDE CORNER

At an outside corner, use a tape measure to measure for the cut in both directions, and mark with a pencil. Score a cut line in both directions. Then repeatedly score the shorter of the lines until you cut all the way through. Bend the cut-out until it snaps off.

Cutting a Notch for a Pipe

When cutting around a pipe, aim to have a ⅛-inch gap between the pipe and the tile. You may have to cut the tile around the pipe into two separate pieces and install each one. After installation, caulk the joint and cover it with a pipe flange.

1 Measure for the notch cut
If only a partial width of tile is needed, cut the tile to width. Hold the tile face up and pressed against the pipe and mark the tile at either side of the pipe. Measure the distance that the tile must travel towards the wall, and add ⅛ inch; this is the depth of the cut.

2 Mark for the cut
Keeping in mind that you want a gap of about ⅛ inch or so around the pipe, draw the outline of the front edge of the pipe.

3 Cut the notch
Carefully score along all the marked lines. Then slice repeatedly until you cut all the way through. Remove and save the cut-out piece. Check the tile for fit; you may need to enlarge the cut slightly.

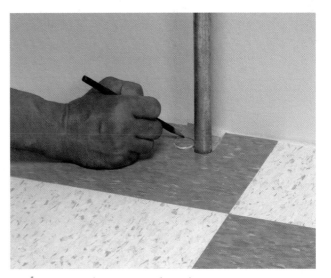

4 Cut the notch piece
Install the tile. Hold the cut-out piece in place, mark it, and cut it to fit behind the pipe. Caulk around the pipe where it meets the tile. Install a pipe flange to cover the caulking, using the kind of flange that opens and closes to fit over existing pipe.

WOOD PARQUET FLOORING

A typical wood parquet tile has tongues and grooves that enable it to fit tightly against adjacent tiles. See page 20 for tips on selecting parquet tiles. These tiles require a special adhesive. Purchase a notched trowel of the size recommended by the adhesive manufacturer. Allow the tiles to sit in the room for at least a day so they can adjust to the ambient temperature and humidity.

Preparing and Laying Out

The substrate for a parquet floor does not need to be very firm, and it does not have to be very smooth. You can install parquet tiles directly over an old wood or vinyl tile floor, as long as it is free of major defects. Remove obstacles and cut moldings (see pages 56–59).

See pages 66–69 for layout instructions. Figuring the layout is easy, because the tiles are exactly 12 inches square, with no grout lines. Wood parquet tiles are laid one small section at a time, so you can start anywhere on the floor; near the center is usually a good choice.

Testing the Tiles for Fit

Before you spread adhesive for a section of tile, set ten or so tiles on the floor and slide them together, as shown above. Check that the edges and corners fit tightly. If two tiles do not fit tightly together, perhaps one has a tongue that is slightly splintered, cut off the offending portion with a knife. Or a groove may be clogged with debris; clean it out with a small screwdriver. Discard tiles that cannot be made to fit.

Setting the Tiles

Sweep the area clear. If the trowel picks up even a small bit of debris, you'll have to remove it. After test-fitting a group of tiles, have them stacked and ready to install; the adhesive sets up quickly. Parquet adhesive is particularly sticky and hard to clean, so keep your hands and knees away from it. Clean up wayward blobs immediately, using a rag soaked with soapy water (for latex-based adhesive) or paint thinner (for oil-based adhesive).

1 Spread the adhesive

Pour some adhesive onto the floor, or scoop it out with the notched trowel. Spread enough adhesive to cover 8 square feet or so. Avoid covering up working lines. Use long, sweeping strokes, and work systematically, so you leave no blobs. Do it right the first time and avoid recombing after a few minutes, because the adhesive starts to harden quickly.

2 Lay the first tile

Set the first tile onto the adhesive at the intersection of the working lines. Push down on it gently, and twist it into perfect alignment. Disregard the tongues when aligning the tile with the working lines.

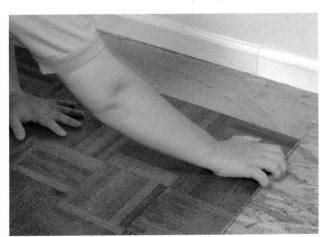

3 Lay more tiles

Set each successive tile next to its neighbor, and slide it into place. You'll be able to slide the tiles around for a half hour or so. Sometimes they'll also move when you don't want them to. Every few minutes, check and adjust the tiles as necessary.

4 Tap together for a tight fit

If the adhesive is starting to set up and some of the seams between tiles are not tight, insert the tongue and groove of a partial tile piece into the groove and tongue of the tile that needs to move, and tap the partial tile with a hammer.

Make sure the tiles are sticking. As long as the adhesive is wet to the touch, the tiles will stick. Once the adhesive starts to skin over (so it feels tacky rather than gooey when you touch it lightly), adhesion will be impaired. To ensure a firm bond, tap each tile with a rubber mallet (right). After tapping, check the alignment of the tiles and adjust if necessary. To test for firm adhesion, attempt to pry up a tile using a margin trowel or a prybar. If the tile refuses to come up after exerting moderate pressure, it is well stuck.

Cutting Tiles

Install the full tiles first. Do not apply adhesive to the floor where the cut tiles will go until a few minutes before you will install them. Cutting parquet tiles is easy if you use a table saw, radial-arm saw, or a power miter box, but cutting them with a circular saw or saber saw is not difficult. Whichever tool you use, keep your fingers well away from the blade. It often helps to clamp the tile onto a work table before cutting it.

Mark for a cut: To measure for a straight cut, place a ¼-inch spacer at the wall (below, left). Set the tile to be cut directly on top of the tile it will slide into. After marking the tile for cutting, transfer the marks to the back of the tile, and cut the tile upside-down to minimize splintering. Place a full tile on top of the tile to be cut, slide it against the spacer, and mark for the cut.

Break apart a tile: If you need a half or a quarter tile, simply bend the parquet until the pieces come apart (below). Sometimes, this is all the cutting you need to do.

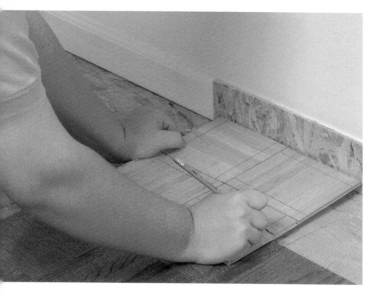

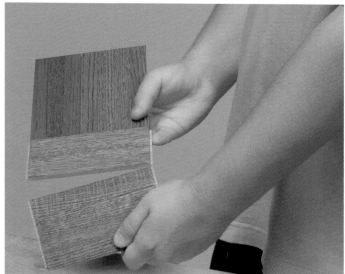

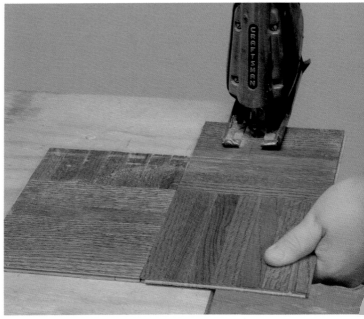

Straight cut with a circular saw: If you cut the tile rightside-up, the circular saw blade may produce unsightly splinters. Instead, transfer the cut line to the back of the tile. Hold the tile firmly in place with your hand against a supporting surface (above), or clamp it to a work table, and make the cut. Be sure to wear eye protection when cutting any tile.

Cut-out with a saber saw: A cut that goes in two directions can be made with a circular saw, but it is easier with a saber saw. As long as you use a fine-cutting blade, you can cut the tile rightside-up. Apply tape to the bottom of the saw baseplate to protect the tile against scratches. Hold or clamp the tile firmly in place (above), and blow away the sawdust as you cut.

CARING FOR A PARQUET FLOOR

Most wood parquet tiles come with a fairly durable protective coating. In theory, if the tiles fit together tightly, the seams will be protected. However, tiles do not always align perfectly, and the protective finish will not last forever.

For a finish that will bead up water for years, add a coat of clear polyurethane once the floor is installed. Oil-based polyurethane is the strongest, but is illegal in some states for environmental reasons; latex-based polyurethane is nearly as strong. Using a hand sander, lightly sand the floor with 180-grit sandpaper. Completely remove all grit so the floor is perfectly clean. Apply the polyurethane using a paint brush or a special applicator. After the finish has dried, sand it lightly.

LAYING LAMINATE TILES

Laminate tiles come in various sizes and shapes, but they all fit together the same way. Two sides of a tile have protruding tongues, and the other two sides have grooves into which tongues fit. Laminate tiles fit together more reliably than wood parquet tiles. If the substrate is smooth and even, and you install laminate tiles correctly, the seams will seal tight and the entire floor will be highly resistant to water damage.

Tile-setting techniques vary slightly from manufacturer to manufacturer, but the steps shown on these pages apply to most installations.

Preparing the Floor

The floor does not have to be particularly firm or smooth, although it must be clean and free of dust and debris. You can install laminate tiles over just about any existing surface, including ceramic or vinyl tile or concrete. Remove obstructions and cut or remove moldings (see pages 56–59).

Rather than snapping working lines and beginning in the middle of a floor (as you would for other types of tile installations), laminate flooring is installed starting at a wall. Begin at a wall that is not out of square. Plan the layout ahead of time (see pages 66–69); you may need to start with cut tiles in order to avoid ending up with narrow tiles at the other end of the room.

Set the tiles, still in their boxes, in the room where they will be installed, and wait two days before installing them. This allows the tiles to adjust to the room temperature and humidity; otherwise, they could expand or contract after installation, creating gaps between tiles or causing the tiles to buckle.

Choose an appropriate foam underlayment for your conditions. For a concrete floor that might get damp, use a product that provides a vapor barrier. Other foam underlayments cushion the floor, deaden noise, or do both.

Roll out the foam underlayment onto the floor in large sections and tape the pieces together as directed by the manufacturer.

Laying the Tiles

Use an installation kit made for your tiles. Some manufacturers recommend that the tiles be clamped together with special straps until the glue sets. The type of installation shown here simply calls for tapping the tiles tightly together.

To cut a laminate tile, turn it upside-down, clamp it to a work table (laminate is quite slippery), and cut the tile with a circular or saber saw.

1 Glue the tiles together
Place spacers against the wall. Set out a dry run of the first three rows, cutting tiles where necessary. Disassemble the section, leaving only the first tile in place. Squirt glue into the groove of the second tile, and slide it into the first one. Use a damp cloth to wipe away the glue that squeezes out. Repeat this process for all the tiles in the first two rows.

2 Tap and tighten
Using the manufacturer's tapping block, gently tap with a hammer to tighten the joints. Wipe away squeezed-up glue, and wait for an hour or so for the glue to set. Repeat this process until you come to the end of the room.

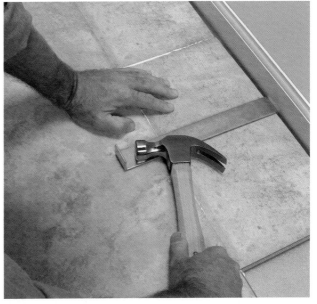

3 Use the pull bar for the last row
To tighten the last row of tiles, tap with a special pull bar. Fit spacers at the wall to hold the tiles tightly in place. After the glue has set, remove the spacers and install moldings and thresholds (see pages 92–93).

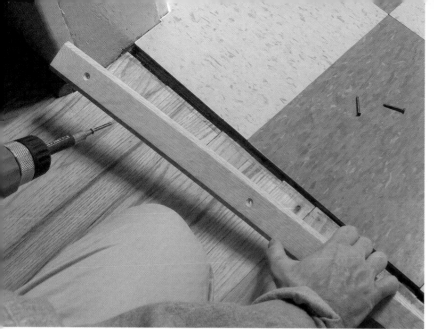

FINISHING THE JOB

Once a new gleaming tile floor has been installed, base moldings that once looked fine may appear shabby. To bring old wood molding up to snuff, fill any holes, sand away imperfections, and apply a fresh coat of paint. You may also want to install new base shoe. If the old molding was vinyl cove base, install new pieces; old pieces never seem to clean up well.

Installing thresholds: Wood thresholds are available in various thicknesses; buy one that will be the same height as the tile, or no more than ⅛ inch lower. If you start with a standard threshold, with tapered edges on either side, you'll have to cut one edge so the full thickness of the threshold butts against the tile.

To install a threshold in a doorway, cut the stop pieces so the threshold can slide under them. Cut the threshold to length, and slide it into position (above, left). Drill pilot holes and drive finish nails to secure the threshold to the floor. Caulk the joint between the threshold and the tiles.

Purchase a marble threshold from a tile supply source, which can cut it to size (above, right). To anchor it to the floor, set it in mortar or silicone adhesive.

If tiles abut a carpeted floor, one option is to purchase an inexpensive metal carpet strip; these are

generally available in shades of bronze or silver. Cut the strip with a pair of tin snips or a hack saw. Set it on top of the joint, drill pilot holes, and drive nails or screws into the floor.

For additional options, as well as guidance in selecting thresholds, see page 63.

Installing base shoe: Sand and paint the old base shoe and install it by driving finish nails through the old nail holes (above). If the nails do not hold well, try using thicker nails. To install new base shoe, use the old pieces as templates for cutting.

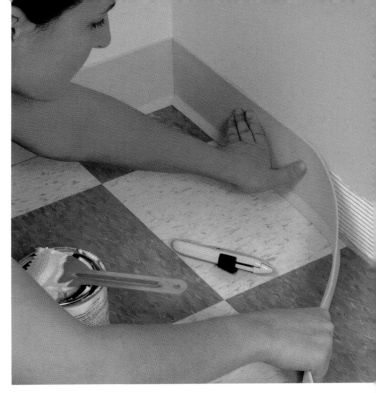

Vinyl cove base: Purchase vinyl cove base that is at least as wide as the old cove base, so it will cover imperfections in the wall. Scrape the wall clean of old adhesive and any protrusions. Using a special cove-base notched trowel, which is just the right width, scoop out cove-base adhesive and apply it to the wall. The adhesive should be applied within an inch of the top of the cove base, but take care not to apply it too high.

Install any outside corner pieces first, then the 4-foot-long pieces. Press the cove base against the wall with your hand, so that the top edge sticks tightly to the wall. When you come to an inside corner, install the first piece tight against the adjacent wall. Cut the other piece square, then nip off a corner at the bottom, so it fits tightly against the other piece. It may take several tries before you get a professional-looking fit.

Sealing tiles and grout: Certain types of unglazed tile should be sealed to protect against staining. Consult with your dealer for the best sealer to apply. Latex-fortified grout is fairly resistant to stain-ing, but a grout sealer will improve its moisture resis-tance and make the floor easier to keep clean.

Consult with your dealer or with the manufacturer for the best way to apply tile and grout sealers. Usually, it is not a good idea to apply grout sealer to the tiles as well. Instead, use a small paint brush or a special appli-cator to apply sealer to the grout only, and wipe the tiles as you go. When applying sealer to tiles, it's usually fine to spread the sealer over the entire area, including the grout lines.

TILE BASE MOLDING

You may be able to purchase base pieces that match the floor tiles in color and length, as shown here. Alternatively, you can install a tile base of a contrasting color. Wait to install the base tiles until after the floor tiles have set, and use thinset mortar or organic mastic. Apply the adhesive to the wall using a narrow trowel, or back butter the base tiles (page 75). Use spacers to position the base pieces the thickness of a grout line above the tiled floor. If the floor is not perfectly level, you may need to fuss with the spacing so that the top edge of the base—the most visible part—is level. Once the adhesive has set, caulk the joint between the base and the floor, and let the caulk dry. Then apply grout between the other tiles.

TILING WALLS

Compared with tiling a floor, applying tiles to a wall is almost easy. The tiles are lighter and easier to cut, you don't have to mix thinset mortar, and you can usually work in a sitting or standing position. However, it's also true that a wall is closer to eye level than a floor, so imperfections will be more apparent.

Aim to install tiles that are in straight rows and that form a consistently even surface. Start by installing a substrate that is smooth and plumb. Time spent straightening out walls will pay off later, because the tiling job will go smoothly, and vertical rows of tiles will be pleasingly parallel with adjacent walls.

Instructions in this chapter emphasize fail-safe methods that enable a homeowner to achieve professional results. Rather than simply snapping working lines and installing tiles against them, for instance, the following pages show how to attach a horizontal batten, which makes it easier to install straight lines of tile. The basic wall project on pages 112–117 shows how to set tiles in organic mastic, which allows you to correct mistakes easily. The tub surround project (see pages 120–129) describes how to set wall tiles in thinset mortar, which is a more challenging task. For the most fool-proof installation, buy self-spacing wall tiles.

A small number of brightly colored tiles can dramatically change the appearance of a room. These 4-by-4 ceramic wall tiles are inexpensive and easy to install.

To create a splashy design like this, break apart the tiles yourself and experiment on a horizontal surface until you achieve a pleasing pattern.

Glass tiles in hues of yellow, orange, and brown make this bathroom a dreamy place. While typically not recommended for floor installations, glass is perfectly suitable for walls and tub enclosures.

The broken tiles in this fireplace surround contrast surprisingly with the antique wood mantle, yet work nicely with the style and colors of the furniture in the room.

A band of dark granite accents a floor of polished travertine tiles. All exposed edges are polished to the same sheen as the tile surfaces.

A grouping of ceramic art tiles fills the small section between the in-wall fireplace and mantle. Cobalt blue visually pops off the stark white wall, making the tile the focal point of the room.

Three metal art tiles form the centerpiece for this one-of-a-kind backsplash. Blue ceramic field tiles and a metal border provide a decorative background and frame.

Black and white ceramic tiles in two sizes distinctively surround this fireplace. Sometimes even a small amount of tile can create a big visual impact.

Beneath a solid marble
bench, a band of
glazed accent tiles runs
through a field of
unglazed Moroccan
terra-cotta tiles.

Slate tiles in different sizes and tones of traditional green, gray, rust, and charcoal meander all around this bathroom.

Colorful ceramic 4-by-4 and 2-by-2 tiles, carefully installed and trimmed with borders, give this shower a well-manicured look. The arched shampoo niche is both decorative and useful.

Large stone tiles in a tranquil neutral color cover the walls and a bench in this spacious shower. The stunning group of glass tiles inset in the wall mimics the glass-block window.

PREPARING A WALL SUBSTRATE

Wall tiles don't get walked on, but they do get bumped, and they can crack if the substrate is weak. New wall tiles strengthen a wall only slightly; don't count on the tiles to tie together a wall with cracks, or to firm up a wall that feels flexible when you press on it.

If the wall to be tiled will be exposed only to occasional moisture, install greenboard (see page 106). If it will get wet regularly, install cement backerboard (see page 122).

Testing and Preparing an Existing Wall Surface

A standard new-home wall, composed of a single layer of ½-inch drywall attached to studs that are spaced 16 inches apart, is just strong enough for most tiling projects. An older plaster wall in good condition is actually stronger.

Test a wall by pressing it with the heel of your hand at various points. If drywall has come loose, drive drywall nails or screws through the drywall and into the studs behind it. For a plaster wall in which plaster has come loose from the underlying lath, you have a more difficult problem. Either remove the plaster (a messy job) and install drywall, or "skin over" the entire surface with a layer of drywall, attached with screws driven into studs. This latter solution raises the surface of the wall, however, so you may have to modify the wall moldings.

To patch a small hole in drywall, purchase a drywall patching kit. For a hole or damaged area larger than 6 inches square, use a drywall saw to cut out a rectangular area around the damage. Cut two 1-by-4 nailers slightly longer than the width of the opening, and

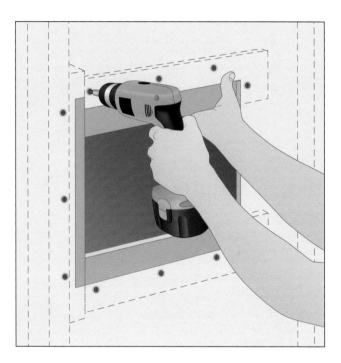

DRYWALL PATCH

PLASTER PATCH

attach them with screws (opposite, top). Cut a piece of drywall to fit, and attach it with screws to the nailers. Apply fiberglass mesh drywall tape and joint compound to the edge of the repair, let it dry, and sand smooth.

To patch a hole or weak spot in a plaster wall, chip out all the loose plaster. Cut a piece of drywall that is the same thickness as the plaster so that it fits approximately in the opening, and attach it to the lath with screws (opposite, bottom). You may need to buy ⅜-inch drywall. Fill the gaps with joint compound, let dry, and sand smooth.

Removing Obstacles

Whenever possible, avoid cutting tiles to fit around an obstruction. You will achieve more professional-looking results—and the job will proceed much more smoothly—if you remove the obstruction and replace it after the tiles have been installed. Detach and remove towel racks, cabinets, and moldings.

If you will be tiling around an electrical switch or receptacle, shut off power to the circuit by switching off a circuit breaker or unscrewing a fuse. Use an electrical tester to make sure the power is off. Remove the cover plate and the screws that hold the switch or receptacle in place, then gently pull it outward. Make sure any wire splices are covered with wire nuts or tape. Wrap electrical tape around exposed screw terminals. Once you are certain the switch or receptacle is safe, you can restore power. Do not use a receptacle while it is pulled out. To reinstall after tiling, see page 117.

If you will be installing tiles directly onto the existing wall surface, scrape away any loose paint. Then use a hand sander to rough up the entire surface to make sure the adhesive will bond firmly.

Check for Plumb and Smoothness

Hold or tape a carpenter's level against a straight board, and hold the board up against the wall near a corner. If a wall is out of plumb, it will not be parallel to a vertical grout line on an adjacent wall. Also test various points along the walls to see if there are any waves. A wave will be most visible if it is near a corner. See page 107 for ways to correct waves or an out-of-plumb wall.

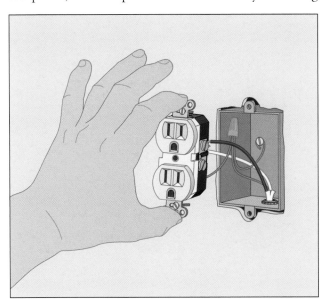

Installing Greenboard

Moisture-resistant drywall, commonly known as greenboard, is usually available in ½-inch-thick 4-foot by 8-foot sheets. The long edges are tapered to accommodate the thickness of the drywall tape and joint compound used to seal the joint. The short edges are not tapered; wherever two non-tapered edges meet in a "butt joint," the thickness of the tape and joint compound will result in a slight outward bump in the wall surface.

Ready-mixed joint compound is easy to apply and sand, but it dries slowly, is not strong, and weakens further if it gets damp. Instead, buy bags of powdered joint compound and mix it with water. The "easy sand" variety is not very strong.

Cut, snap, and cut again: Measure for the cut, and subtract ¼ inch. A drywall square makes quick work of scoring square lines across the width of a sheet. Hold the square firmly against the cut line, and use a utility knife to score a line (below). Bend the sheet back until it snaps, then cut through the back side to complete the cut.

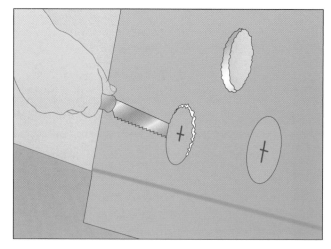

Cut holes with a drywall saw: If you need to cut a hole, first measure and mark the shape. Score the outline with a utility knife, using a straightedge for any linear cuts. Cut the hole with a drywall saw (above); keep the saw to the inside of the line as you cut.

Attach the greenboard: Use the drywall square to draw lines indicating the centers of studs. Hold the sheet in place up against the studs (a helper will make this easier), and drive screws into the studs. Each screw head must dimple the surface inward, but not so far that it breaks the paper, or it will lose holding power.

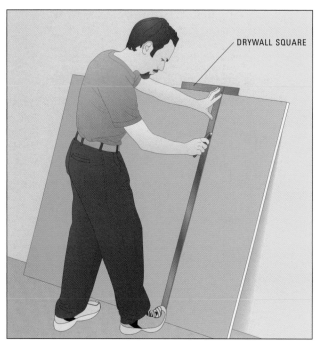

DRYWALL SQUARE

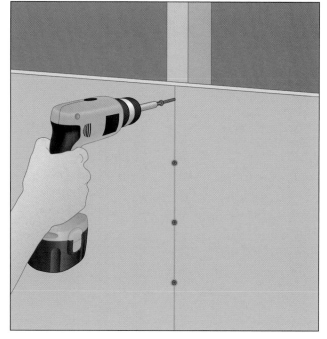

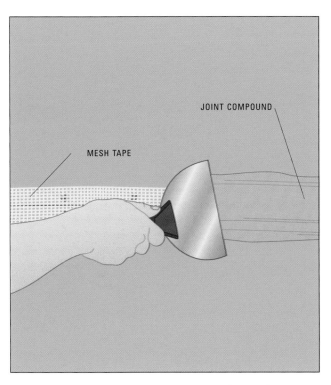

JOINT COMPOUND

MESH TAPE

Tape the joints: Cut and apply mesh tape to the joints. Mix a batch of joint compound until it is smooth, and use a 6- or 8-inch taping blade to spread the compound over the tape. Allow the compound to dry, and scrape away any protrusions. Apply another coat or two, let dry, and sand smooth.

Straightening a Wall

If a wall has serious waves near the corners or is more than ½ inch out of plumb, take steps to straighten things out.

Shimming: If a wall is out of plumb, use a level to draw a plumb line next to it on the adjacent wall. Every 8 inches or so along the out-of-plumb stud (or wall, if you are skinning over it), nail a shim that is thick enough to come up to the plumb line. (Cut shims with a utility knife.) Hold a level against the shims to double-check for plumb. On the adjacent wall, draw arrows pointing to the thickest parts of the shim. When you install greenboard or backerboard, drive screws at those points.

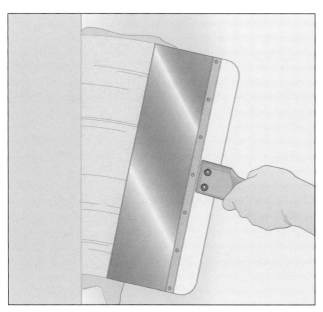

Adjusting with joint compound: To correct concavities in an existing wall, or to bring a wall into plumb, you can use joint compound, a 12-inch-wide taping knife (above), and plenty of patience. Apply joint compound, and spread it with the taping knife so it looks fairly straight. Check your work with a straightedge, a level, or both, and make adjustments as necessary. After the compound dries, sand it smooth and check again. It may take several applications to make the wall smooth and plumb.

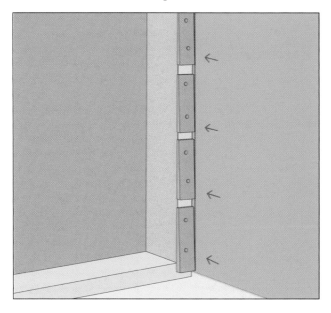

Preparing Other Wall Surfaces

A substrate for wall tiles must be stable so it will not expand and contract during changes of temperature or humidity. It must also be able to grip the adhesive; organic mastic or thinset adhesive is likely to come loose from a surface that is glossy or oily.

Keep in mind that the adhesive does not stick to the underlying wall material, but to the surface. For instance, if paint is likely to peel (as with latex paint on top of oil-based paint), the tile adhesive will peel off as well, dislodging the tiles.

Wallpaper: By design, wallpaper paste is weak; it's just strong enough to hold the paper. Strip all the wallpaper (there may be several layers) before tiling. Remove wallpaper even if it has been painted over.

Existing tile: Even if existing wall tile is firmly attached, there are two problems to overcome. First, the glazed surface may be too slick for adhesive to adhere. The glazes on wall tiles are usually soft, however, and can be roughed up with a belt sander (below). Second, an extra layer of tiles will stick out from the wall, meaning that you'll have to find a special way to finish the edges. Radius bullnose may be the solution (see the illustration on page 120).

Wood paneling: All types of wood paneling—from cheap sheets with a wood-grain veneer to solid tongue-and-groove planks—expand and contract with changes in the weather. Do not tile over wood of any sort. Instead, remove the paneling and patch the underlying wall.

Concrete: A basement wall made of concrete may be a suitable surface for tiling. Chances are it will not be smooth; use a grinder to level any bumps. Scrub the wall with a concrete cleaner to be sure all oils are removed, then brush on liquid concrete bonding agent. Keep in mind that basement walls often develop cracks after a decade or two. To protect the tiles from cracking, install an isolation membrane (see pages 64–65).

Brick or block: Tile adhesive will have no trouble gripping the rough surface of brick or concrete block. However, masonry walls are usually uneven, making it difficult to install a smooth tile surface. Straighten out a masonry wall by applying a skim coat of brick mortar mixed with extra Portland cement. If a powdery white substance (called efflorescence) appears on a brick wall, or if bricks are crumbling, consult with a mason before tiling.

LAYING OUT FOR WALL TILE

Once you have prepared the walls and made sure they are plumb and flat (see pages 104–108), it's time to plan exactly where the tiles will go. The main goal when laying out wall tile is to avoid a row of very narrow cut tiles. Narrow tiles look awkward and emphasize any imperfections in adjoining walls. A secondary goal is symmetry: whenever possible, center the tiles on the wall, so that the cut tiles at either side are the same size.

An obstruction such as a window can make the layout much more complicated, because you also need to avoid having narrow tiles around three (or even four) sides of the window.

Install a Batten and Make a Dry Run

Decide how high the second horizontal row of tiles will be above the floor. If the floor beneath is fairly level and the bottom of the tiles will be covered with a base molding, position the second row above the floor by the height of one tile plus an inch or so. If there will be no base molding, and the bottom row of tiles must meet the floor precisely, plan to cut all the bottom-row tiles to about three-fourths height.

Use a level to draw a working line for the second row, and also draw a plumb line in the exact center of the room.

Attach a batten—a very straight board—with its top edge against the horizontal line. A long strip of plywood with one factory edge makes an ideal batten.

Position tiles in a dry run on top of the batten, starting at the center line and running to one adjacent wall. If the tiles are not self-spacing, place spacers between them. If this layout leads to a narrow cut tile at the end, mark a corrected vertical working line, moving it by the width of half a tile in either direction.

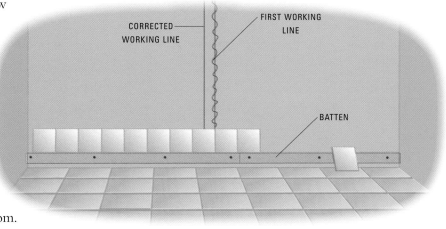

CORRECTED WORKING LINE

FIRST WORKING LINE

BATTEN

Bullnose

Border

Last Row

Soap
Dish

Mark for Top of the Installation and Accessories

If the tiles will not reach to the ceiling, decide where to position the top of the installation. Make a jury stick (see page 68) and hold it vertically to mark for the courses of field tiles, borders (if any), and the bullnose pieces at the top.

Soap dishes, toilet paper holders, towel racks, and other accessories typically are mounted to the wall after the tiles have been set. Choose accessories that fit into the space of one tile, or else set cut tiles to accommodate them. To make sure you remember to leave space for an accessory, mark its location on the wall.

Designing Around Obstacles

Small obstacles such as electrical receptacles or switches are not usually considered in the layout; an occasional narrow cut tile is not a problem. However, if an obstacle is large and at eye level, it may be the focal point of the wall. In that case, it's important to avoid narrow cut tiles around it, and preferable to make the cut tiles on either side the same size.

Use a jury stick to determine whether there will be a narrow horizontal row of tiles just below or above the obstacle. If so, you may choose to raise or lower the batten. Also check to see if there will be a narrow vertical row of tiles along either edge of the obstacle. If so, you may have to choose between narrow tiles there or at the wall edges.

The molding piece below a window sill, called the apron, can be removed and replaced after the tiles have been set. You can also remove it permanently and tile all the way up to the window sill. No other window moldings can be treated this way.

If a room has more than one highly visible obstruction, you'll probably have to make some compromises. If any of the obstructions is seriously out of plumb or level, try to place wide cut tiles there.

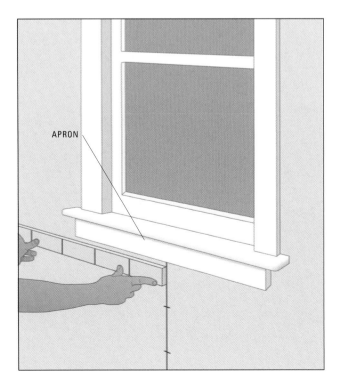

APRON

DECORATIVE BORDERS

The most popular way to enliven a wall of tiles is to run a decorative border along the top, and perhaps along the sides as well. Three such borders are shown here. Tile brochures, as well as tile stores and home centers, offer quite a few design and color suggestions. While these are often a good place to start, you should feel free to make up your own design. To be safe, buy all the tiles from the same manufacturer, so they will fit together.

Carefully think through the entire layout; it helps to make a detailed drawing, using graph paper. One simple but effective border uses a row of thin tiles and a finish cap, with a row of field tiles sandwiched between. To add more interest, use strips of mosaics, tiles tilted to look like diamonds, or triangular tiles.

TILING A WALL

If the wall substrate is well prepared, installing the tiles will be a straightforward job. Double-check to see that the surface is flat and firm, and that adjoining walls are plumb.

Organic mastic comes ready-mixed, is easy to apply, and allows tiles to be adjusted as much as an hour after installation. Thinset is more difficult to work with, but it is more resistant to water. Use mastic for walls that will stay relatively dry, and consider thinset for a wall that will often get wet, such as a tub enclosure (see page 126).

1 Apply mastic

Using a trowel with notches recommended by the mastic manufacturer, scoop mastic out of the tub and spread it on the wall. Do not cover the working lines. As much as possible, apply the mastic with long, sweeping strokes. Hold the trowel at the same angle all the time, to ensure a setting bed of consistent depth. The trowel's teeth should lightly scrape the wall surface.

2 Install tiles

Press each tile into the adhesive. Avoid sliding a tile more than a half inch. Add spacers as you go. Every 15 minutes or so, check the entire installation to make sure no tiles have strayed out of alignment. Using a cloth dampened with water or mineral spirits (depending on the type of mastic used), wipe away any mastic that squeezes onto the surface of a tile.

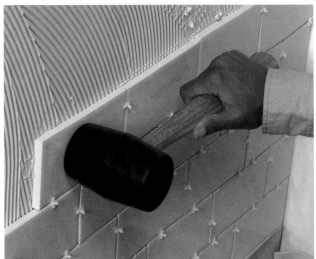

3 Bed the tiles

Tap the tile surface with a mallet to make sure the tiles are embedded in the mastic and to form a smooth wall surface. If a tile's surface is raised noticeably above the surface of its neighbor, try tapping it tighter against the wall using a rubber mallet. If this doesn't do the trick, you may have to remove some tiles, reapply mastic, and start again.

Installing Irregular Tiles

If the tiles are precisely made, simply set spacers in each corner. However, if the tiles are not consistent in shape or size, you will have to improvise. Depending on how irregular they are, you may choose to use standard spacers, and turn some of them sideways, as shown above. With some some tiles, you can adjust spacing by pushing the spacers in or pulling them outward. Other options include scraps of cardboard (see page 115) or wedge-shaped plastic tile spacers. Whichever method you use, check every other row or so to see that the tiles form a reasonably straight horizontal line.

Installing Brick-Shaped Tiles

If brick tiles are installed one on top of two, as shown at right, draw two vertical working lines near the center of the wall, representing the leading edges of alternating courses.

Cutting Wall Tiles

Most ceramic wall tiles are softer than floor tiles and can be easily cut with a snap cutter or rod saw. If a ceramic tile is too hard for a rod saw, use a wet saw, nippers, or both together (see pages 70–71). Stone tiles must always be cut with a wet saw.

To make a cutout with a rod saw, hold the tile firmly in place, with the area to be cut overhanging the work surface (right). Saw with steady, moderate pressure. It is easy to turn corners with a rod saw.

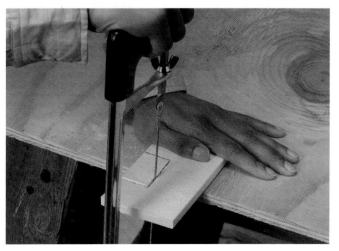

Accessories

Soap dishes, towel racks, toothpaste holders, and toilet paper holders get pulled and bumped. Some installers choose a strong adhesive as a result, such as thinset mortar or, as shown in this project, silicone adhesive. Others deliberately use a weak adhesive such as organic mastic so that the piece will pop out as a unit rather than breaking if someone leans or pulls too hard on it.

Some accessories are designed to be attached to the wall substrate, while others go on the tile surface. Still others attach via plates that are screwed to the tiles (see page 185). More details can be found on pages 124–125.

Self-Spacing Tiles

Some tiles, such as those shown in the photo at right, have two nubs on each edge, so that when the tiles are butted together there is a perfect grout line between them. Installing these self-spacing tiles is quick and easy. If a cut tile of this type is slightly larger than it should be, don't force it in; cut a new tile, or reduce the size of the cut tile using a tile stone.

MOSAIC WALL TILE

Setting mosaic tile in a bed of thinset mortar is tricky and messy (see page 79). It's easier to install mosaics in organic mastic. Tap the tiles with a beater block, or push with the heel of your hand, and wipe away any mastic that squeezes out. Mosaics are ideal for curved surfaces; the smaller the individual tiles, the tighter the curves they can accommodate.

Trim Tiles

Unless you are installing stone tile, exposed edges should be bullnose pieces (also called "caps"), which have one finished edge. At an outside corner, use a corner piece or a "down angle" tile, which has two finished edges. For more information on trim tiles, see page 31. To install a border, see page 128.

If the bullnose tiles are supposed to have the same dimensions as the field tiles, don't be surprised if they are slightly smaller; just leave a bit more space between them in order to maintain straight grout lines. If the bullnose pieces are sized differently from the field tiles, decide whether you want some of the grout lines to match up; usually, it looks better if none do.

1 Apply the mastic
Spread the mastic right up to the edge line of the area to be tiled, but no farther. All the tile should be embedded in mastic, but any excess mastic must be cleaned away.

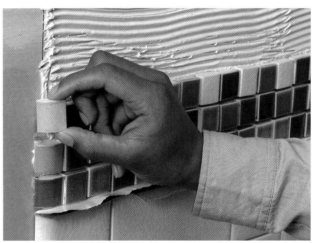

2 Install bullnose pieces
Set the caps just as you did the field tiles, and press or tap with a beater block to make sure they stick to the mastic.

3 Install the corner piece
Wherever two edges will be exposed, install a down angle tile or a decorative corner tile.

4 Wipe clean
Using a rag dampened with water or mineral spirits, depending on the type of mastic, thoroughly wipe away all excess mastic.

Grouting

Use unsanded grout for joints less than ⅛ inch wide, and sanded grout for wider joints. Unless the grout is fortified with powdered latex, mix it with liquid latex even if the directions say you can mix it with water only.

Prepare as much grout as you can use in 20 minutes or so. In a clean bucket, mix the liquid with the powder (a margin trowel works well as a mixing tool) until the grout is free of lumps and about as thick as toothpaste. Wait 10 minutes, then stir again.

1 Push grout into place

Scoop grout out of the bucket with a laminated grout float, and smear it onto the wall. Working in sections about 4 feet square, push the grout into the spaces between the tiles. Hold the float nearly flat and sweep the float diagonally across the tile surface, so it does not dig in. At all points, press the grout in by moving the float systematically in at least two directions.

2 Scrape the excess

Tilt the float up and use it like a squeegee to wipe away most of the grout from the face of the tiles. Scrape diagonally, so the edge of the float cannot dig into the grout lines.

3 Wipe the surface

Dampen a sponge, and wipe the tiles gently. Rinse the sponge every few minutes with clean water. If you see a gap in a grout line, push grout into the gap using your finger, and wipe away the excess. Wipe the surface two or three times.

4 Make even joints

Run the sponge gently along all the vertical lines, then along the horizontal lines, to achieve grout lines of consistent width and depth. If you're having trouble making consistent lines, try tooling the joint by running a rounded handle like this one along each line. Allow the grout to dry, then buff the surface of the tiles with a dry, lint-free cloth.

Caulking

Even if your grout is not white, a tile center may sell a caulk that matches it. Pure silicone caulk is the easiest to keep clean; silicone-reinforced latex caulk will dull if wiped often. "Tub and tile" caulk performs almost as well as silicone.

Making clean caulk lines is a skill that you can learn quickly. Practice on scrap pieces until you feel you can control the flow of caulk and make a line of consistent thickness. For another caulking method, see page 129.

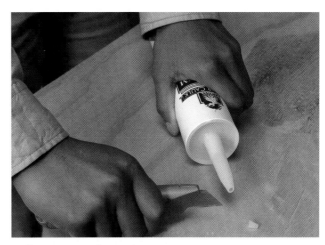

1 Cut the tip

With a utility knife, cut off the tip of the caulking tube's nozzle. The closer to the tip you cut, the thinner the bead of caulk will be. Some people like to cut at a steep angle, while others cut the tip almost straight across. With some caulking tubes, you also need to poke a long nail or a wire down through the nozzle to break a seal.

2 Apply the caulk

Squeeze the caulking gun's trigger until caulk starts to come out; push down on the release button to stop the flow. Place the nozzle tip on the joint to be caulked, squeeze the trigger, and move the nozzle along the joint as you continue to squeeze.

3 Tool the joint

If you manage to squeeze out a line of caulk that is pleasingly straight and smooth, you could just leave it. For a more finished look, dampen a rag or sponge with water or mineral spirits. Wad it up and run it along the caulk line to make a smooth joint.

REPLACING ELECTRICAL DEVICES

Shut off power to the circuit supplying the switch or receptacle. If the electrical box is recessed more than $\frac{1}{4}$ inch, insert a box extender into the electrical box. Screw the device to the box; its ears should rest on top of the tiles. Replace the coverplate, and restore power.

Tumbled limestone, in 4-by-4 tiles, covers the walls of this bathroom from floor to ceiling.

INSTALLING STONE TILE ON WALLS

Stone wall tile—either polished or rough—can usually be installed on any wall suitable for ceramic tile. Most stone tiles should be set in thinset mortar rather than organic mastic (see page 136). Make all the cuts with a wet saw.

Some types of natural stone stain easily, and some are translucent. Use white thinset when installing light-colored marble or other stone; gray thinset or brown organic mastic can subtly muddy the stone's color. If you choose a grout that is not similar in color to the stone, check with the tile supplier to make sure the grout will not stain the stone.

Natural stone varies from tile to tile in color and pattern. Examine tiles from all the boxes, laying them out based on color and thickness. You may choose to "shuffle" the tiles, so there will be an even distribution of tiles with certain characteristics.

Polished Tiles

Stately tiles made of polished marble, granite, or other stone are usually large—12 inches square—and are installed with very thin grout lines. This means that the tiles must all be installed perfectly flat, so that the entire surface is smooth and even.

Installation techniques are not much different than for other types of wall tile, except that you have to be especially careful and precise. Diligently examine the substrate. Check walls to see that they are precisely flat and smooth, and correct even the most minor imperfections. Spread the mortar holding the trowel at the same angle at all times, so the setting bed is a consistent depth. Constantly check and recheck that the surfaces of adjacent tiles are on the same plane. Don't be surprised if you have to remove a tile and reset it in order to achieve a smooth wall.

If any tile edges will be exposed, they must be finished ahead of time, so they are as shiny as the tile surface. The best way is to have them professionally buffed; a tile dealer may know a place where this can be done. If you'd like to try a do-it-yourself method, you can sand the edges with very fine sandpaper, then brush on two or more coats of clear lacquer. Or use a grinder, as shown on page 136.

Exposed edges on this stone tile tub surround are polished to the same high sheen as the tile surface.

Exposed edges of tumbled marble tiles are left rough for a weathered look.

Rough Stone Tiles

More and more bathroom walls are being covered with large, rustic-looking rough tiles made of limestone, marble or slate. In most respects, the installation is much easier than for smooth tiles. A slightly uneven surface is generally considered fine or even desirable, and the edges do not have to be polished.

The only potential concern is the weight of the tiles. If a tile is not firmly embedded in thinset of the correct consistency, it could fall out during installation. There's no need to brace tiles temporarily; just make sure they are well set.

TILING A TUB ENCLOSURE

A tub enclosure is one of the most common tiling projects. In most cases, the tile extends about 4 feet above the tub. On the sides, you can either stop the tile at the edge of the tub (see page 128) or extend the tile surface past the tub so that a row of trim tiles reaches to the floor.

Choosing the Ensemble

Purchase bullnose tiles for the outside edges along the top and the sides of the installation. You'll probably need two outside corner pieces, which have bullnose edges on two sides. See page 31 for trim options.

One common border, as depicted on page 126, combines outside trim pieces and thin liner pieces, with a row of field tiles sandwiched in between. The thin trim pieces may turn a corner and run vertically down the sides (see page 128), or can run horizontally only, meeting the vertical outside trim.

Preparing the Substrate

Use cement backerboard as a substrate. Many tub enclosures are tiled using greenboard for the substrate. These installations can last a long time, as long as the grout and caulk are kept in perfect condition, with no holes. However, if even a small gap develops in the grout or caulk of a tub enclosure, the substrate will eventually get soaked. Greenboard (or worse yet, standard drywall) will then crumble and fall apart.

Adhesive options: Thinset mortar stays strong when it gets wet; organic mastic weakens in time if it is left damp. However, thinset is more difficult to work with, because it must be kept not too wet and not too dry. If you don't feel confident using thinset (see page 126), switch to organic mastic, and afterward take special care to maintain the caulk and grout lines.

Protecting the tub: Demolition and tiling can easily scratch a tub. Cut pieces of rosin paper (also called construction paper) to fit tightly, so the paper does not rip while you work. Seal the paper with wide masking tape. Place a dropcloth on the bottom of the tub, and position a piece of plywood, about 2 feet by 3 feet, on top of the tub to catch falling debris.

If you trim out with radius bullnose tiles, you can skip the step of removing the existing substrate. Install cement backerboard onto the surface of the wall; the radius bullnose pieces will wrap around the backerboard at the edges.

Removing plumbing: Faucet handles attach in different ways. In most cases, you first need to pry off a decorative cover in the center of the handle, using a butter knife or a small screwdriver. Loosen and remove the screw underneath, and pull off the handle. If there is an escutcheon (flange) behind the handle, it may simply lift off, or you may have to loosen a small setscrew first.

To remove a spout without damaging its finish, stick a wooden dowel (a hammer handle made of wood will also work) into the opening, and turn counterclockwise. Otherwise, wrap the faucet with tape or a rag, and use slip-joint pliers or a pipe wrench. Use the same technique to remove a shower arm.

Removing tiles and substrate: Depending on how they were installed, it may be easy or very difficult to take out the old tiles and substrate. Try removing tiles with a flat prybar and a hammer. If the tiles were set in a thick mortar bed, you may need a cold chisel and plenty of time.

Once the tiles are off, mark the wall to show the outline of the new tiled surface, and remove the substrate to within an inch or two of the line. (If you go past the line, you will need to patch the wall—a time-consuming process.) For a plaster wall, either remove the wood lath along with the plaster, or remove only the plaster. Inspect the studs you have just exposed, and make any necessary repairs if some are rotten.

TARPAPER MEMBRANE

For an extra measure of protection for your framing, staple roofing felt (also called tarpaper) to the studs. Because it is saturated with tar, the paper will self-seal when you drive screws through it while installing the backerboard.

Installing Cement Backerboard

Remove all nails or screws from the studs. Measure to find out how thick the backerboard must be in order to match the surrounding wall surface. See page 61 for complete instructions on cutting backerboard.

Install the backerboard on the back wall first, then on the side walls. For the side wall with plumbing, cut holes for the pipes as shown in step 3, then install the backerboard piece the same way. The side-wall backerboard must be flush with the abutting wall surface.

1 Cut and place on spacers

Place small strips of ¼-inch plywood on the rim of the tub as spacers. This creates a gap between the tub and the backerboard that you will fill with caulk. Without this gap, moisture could wick up into the backerboard if the caulking ever fails, which could damage the studs.

Starting with the back wall, cut pieces of backerboard to fit, allowing an ⅛-inch gap between pieces. Drive just a few backerboard screws through the backerboard and into the studs. Make sure the heads of the screws are sunk just below the surface of the backerboard.

2 Check for plumb

If a wall is out of plumb, the vertical row of tiles on the adjacent wall will not be parallel. For a wall that is more than ¼ inch out of plumb, remove the backerboard and install shims (see page 107). Replace the backerboard and drive screws every 6 inches into the studs.

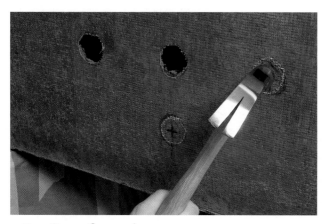

3 Cut for pipes

Measure and mark the backerboard for the center of each pipe. Drill each hole using a carbide-tipped hole saw about ¼ inch wider than the pipe. Alternatively, drill a small hole in the center using a masonry bit, then score the outline of the hole using a backerboard knife; repeat on the other side. Punch the hole out with a hammer.

4 Tape the joints

Press fiberglass mesh tape along each joint. Mix a little thinset mortar (see page 125), and trowel a thin coat over the mesh tape. Feather the edges and smooth any bumps.

Laying Out the Job

In general, lay out the walls for tiling as described on pages 109–111, but adapt the process for a tub enclosure as described below. If you will be tiling around a window, see pages 130–131.

For a bathtub that is perfectly level in both directions, you can install full-sized tiles running horizontally at the bottom. If the tub is slightly out of level, install a bottom row of half- or three-quarter-sized tiles; this will allow you to cut some larger than others.

On each wall, install a batten—a perfectly straight board that is attached to the wall so that it is level and can support the second horizontal row of tiles (shown below). Secure the battens with screws driven into the studs.

You may want to do a vertical dry run of tiles to find out where the top of the installation will be. Then do a horizontal dry run: set as many full tiles as possible on the battens, with spacers if you will be using them, and adjust them as needed. On the back wall, it's important that the vertical rows of cut tiles at either end be the same size. On the side walls, determine where you want the installation to end, then use the dry run to check the size of the cut tiles at the inside corners; you may need to adjust the layout so the cut tiles will be at least half size.

Once the dry-run tiles are where you want them, draw layout lines. Mark the back wall at a grout line near the center of the wall, and on each side wall, mark where the bullnose pieces will end. Remove the tiles, and use a level to draw plumb lines running up from those three marks. Use a framing square to make sure that the lines are perfectly square with the batten.

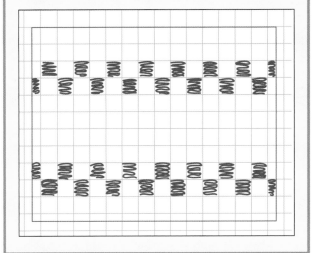

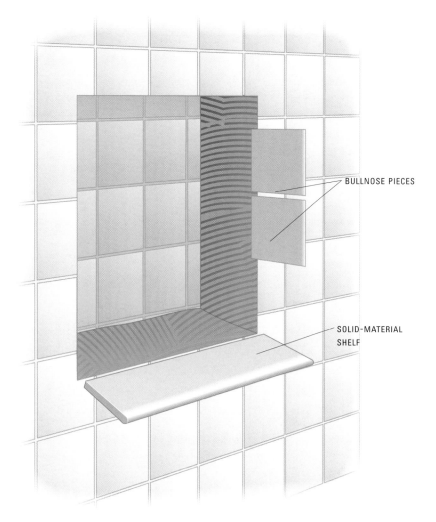

BULLNOSE PIECES

SOLID-MATERIAL SHELF

way, the shelf will tilt slightly downward for water drainage. Cut and install bullnose tiles along the inside edges of the opening to create finished corners. The bullnose pieces just above the shelf need to be cut at a slight angle because of the tilt in the shelf. Fill in remaining spaces with field tiles.

An integrated soap dish: Some soap dishes are attached to the surface of a tiled wall, while others, like the one shown here, are set flush with the tile surface. A soap dish is not meant to be used as a handle for pulling yourself up out of the tub. Some installers prefer to attach a soap dish using a weak adhesive such as organic mastic so the dish will pop out in one piece, rather than break, if it is pulled hard.

Planning Special Features

It's not difficult to add customized features to a tub enclosure as long as you plan ahead. Some features can be added as you tile, while others require that you build in the needed supports or spacing when you install the framing and backerboard.

A shampoo niche: Purchase a shelf made of solid material, available at tile centers. Some types can be cut with a circular saw; others require a wet saw. Before you install the backerboard, cut two 2-by-4 crosspieces to fit between the studs that are at each side of the planned niche, and use 3-inch screws to install one crosspiece above and one below. Bear in mind that after the backerboard and tiles are installed, the finished opening will be about 1½ inches smaller in either direction than the framed opening. Cover the sides and back of the opening with backerboard.

When you tile the wall, cut and install tiles that go right to the edges of the opening. Cut the shelf to fit. Spread mortar on the bottom side of the opening so the mortar is thicker at the back than at the front; that

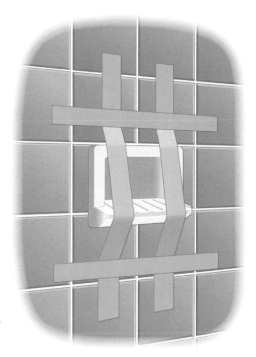

If possible, purchase a soap dish that is the same size as the tiles. That way, you can simply leave one tile out, and install the dish in the resulting opening. Otherwise, you will need to cut tiles to create an opening of the correct size. As you tile, hold the soap dish in place, to make sure it will fit.

Install the soap dish after the tiles have set, either before or after grouting. Place four pieces of masking tape within easy reach. Butter the back of the soap dish with thinset, organic mastic, or silicone adhesive. Push the dish into position, and wipe away any adhesive that oozes out. Use the pieces of masking tape to hold the dish in place while the adhesive sets.

A shower seat: A triangular shower seat does not need to be recessed into the substrate; installing it between two rows of tiles holds it firmly. The row of tiles directly below the seat must be cut ahead of time to accommodate the thickness of the seat. Experiment to find the precise height of these tiles, so that after the seat is installed the row of tiles directly above it will be at the correct height. Note that the tiles on either side must be notch-cut so they fit tightly against the corner of the seat. Apply silicone adhesive to the back edges of the seat, and slip the seat into place against the backerboard. Allow the silicone to set for several hours before installing the rest of the tiles.

Mixing Thinset for Wall Tile

In a small bucket about 2 gallons in size, combine thinset powder with latex additive (see page 73) to make enough thinset to last for 20 minutes or so. Hand-mix it with a margin trowel, or use a small mixer on an electric drill, until all the lumps are gone and the mortar is about the thickness of mayonnaise. It should be almost thick enough to stick to a trowel held sideways, but not quite.

Wait for 10 minutes, then stir again. The mixture will be a bit thicker. Ideally, the mortar should be just stiff enough to hold the shape of trowel lines on the wall, but wet enough so that you are sure tiles will stick to it.

If the mortar starts to harden while you are installing tiles, throw the batch out and mix a new batch. Every once in a while, pull a tile out of the mortar and check that the mortar is sticking firmly.

Setting Tiles

See that the batten is level and the layout lines are plumb. Tiles set in organic mastic can be adjusted up to 15 minutes after setting them, but tiles set in thinset mortar should not be moved after 5 minutes. Check the tiles for alignment every few minutes.

To install irregularly shaped tiles, check every other horizontal row of tiles for level, and follow the plumb layout line in the center of the wall closely. Use scraps of cardboard as spacers, perhaps getting them from the tile box; fold over if a wider space is needed.

If you are installing regularly shaped tiles that are not self-spacing, place a plastic spacer at every corner, as shown here for the field tiles. Self-spacing tiles (see page 114) simply butt against each other. With either type of tile, once you have installed ten tiles or so, there is no way to change the alignment. Don't worry if the tiles go slightly awry from the layout line; it's more important that the tile corners align with each other.

Start cutting tiles: Cut tiles with a snap cutter or a wet saw (see pages 70–71). Before you start installing tiles on the back wall, cut three or four tiles to fit at the edges, and leave the cutting guide in position so that you can quickly cut more. The cut tiles on the back wall can be as much as ¼ inch short; the ends will be covered by the thickness of the side wall tiles.

Install field tiles on the back wall: Using a ¼-by-¼ square-notched trowel, spread thinset over about 10 square feet of the wall. Do not cover up the layout line. Starting with tiles that rest on the batten, press tiles firmly into the mortar. Install the cut tiles on either side as you go. To make sure the tiles will stick, back-butter each piece with a thin coat of mortar.

Finish the back wall: Install all the tiles above the batten for the back wall, including the cut pieces at the corners, the border (if any), and the bullnose tiles at the top. Then move on to the side walls.

1 Measure around a pipe
Install the full-sized tiles closest to a pipe, then hold a tile in place and mark it for a cut. Use a square to mark both sides of the notch.

Tile the side walls: On the side wall with no plumbing, install the first two rows of full-sized field tiles, then measure and cut pieces to fit at the corner. These must be cut precisely: there should be no more than a ¹⁄₁₆-inch gap at the corner, but you should not have to force a tile into place. If a tile is slightly too wide, use a tile stone to shave off a little, or cut a new tile. Keep the tile-cutting guide in position, so you can easily cut tiles for the next rows. You may need to adjust the cutting guide slightly as you move up the wall. Finish with the border and trim tiles as for the back wall.

On the side wall with plumbing, install as many full-sized tiles as possible. Temporarily prop any unsupported tiles so they stay in horizontal alignment. Then measure for the tiles that must be cut to go around the pipes.

2 Cut the tile
Most wall tiles can be cut using a rod saw. A grinder, wet saw, or nibbling tool also works (see page 71). Make the cut about ¼ larger than it needs to be.

Tiling Around Pipes

In most cases, you will need to cut a notch in a tile to go around a pipe, as shown at right. If a pipe falls in the middle of a tile, measure to the center of the pipe, and bore a hole using a drill equipped with a carbide-tipped hole saw.

3 Install the tile
Test that no part of the tile ends up closer than ⅛ inch to the pipe. If the mortar on the substrate has begun to harden while you were cutting the tile, scrape the mortar away and back-butter the tile.

Tiling Near the Tub

The bottom row of tiles should be ⅛ inch above the tub, to prevent cracking if the area expands and contracts due to changes in temperature. Cutting the tile located near the outer edge of the tub also requires special care.

Installing the bottom row: Remove the batten, and scrape away any dried thinset. Cut tiles to fit, allowing for the ⅛-inch gap above the tub. If possible, spread thinset on the wall; otherwise, back-butter the tiles and press them into place.

Cutting at the corner: The bullnose tile at each outer corner of the tub could be cut straight like the others, but you'll achieve a neater appearance if you curve-cut it to follow the curve of the tub. Cutting this piece is tricky, so prepare a cardboard template with a utility knife. Trace the outline onto a bullnose tile, and cut carefully with a rod saw.

Finishing

Wait overnight, then remove any spacers. Wherever the mortar is less than ¼ inch below the surface of the tile, dig it out with a grout saw, small screwdriver, or utility knife; otherwise, the mortar may show through the grout. Clean all mortar off the surface of the tiles using a damp cloth or a scrubbing tool.

Grouting: Purchase sanded grout for tiles spaced apart by ⅛ inch or more, and unsanded grout for narrower grout lines. If the grout powder does not contain latex additives, mix it with liquid latex rather than water.

Follow manufacturer's instructions for mixing the grout; you may need to mix an entire box or bag at once in order to ensure uniformity of color. Add liquid in small amounts at a time and mix by hand in a bucket, using a margin trowel or a putty knife, until the grout is just liquid enough to pour. Wait 10 minutes, and stir again. If it is too stiff, add a little more liquid.

Scoop the grout out of the bucket with a laminated grout float, and push the grout into the lines between the tiles with the float held nearly flat. Move the float in at least two different directions at every point, to ensure that the grout is really pushed in. Once grout has been pushed into an area about 10 feet square, tilt the float up at a steep angle so you can use it as a squeegee. Scrape away most of the excess grout, moving the float at an angle so the float cannot dig into the grout lines.

TILING DOWN TO THE FLOOR

On the side walls, you may choose to extend the tiles past the tub by the width of a tile or two, in which case the outermost tiles will extend down to the floor. In that case, remove the baseboard trim, install the tiles, and cut and install the baseboard to meet the tiles.

After you have grouted a wall, lightly clean the surface with a large, damp sponge. Turn the sponge over when it gets caked with grout, and rinse the sponge often in clean water. Once all the walls have been grouted, rub the surface lightly with the sponge to achieve grout lines that are uniform in depth and width. If any gaps appear, push in a little grout with your finger and rub with the sponge again.

Sponge the surface one last time, then allow the grout to dry for a day. After the grout is dry, buff the tile surface with a clean, dry cloth until it shines. Seal the grout.

Caulking: The caulk line where the tile meets the tub is critical, both for appearance and for protection of the substrate. You could simply squirt a line of caulk and tool it with your finger (see page 117). For a more professional appearance, use the masking tape method (right).

Before caulking, remove the protective covering from the tub, clean the tile and the tub where the caulk will go, and dry thoroughly. Purchase a "tub and tile" caulk that matches the color of your grout.

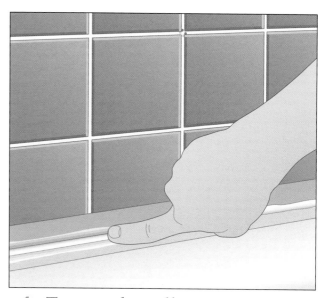

1 Tape and caulk
Apply a piece of masking tape along either side of the joint. Caulk the joint, then smooth the caulk with your finger.

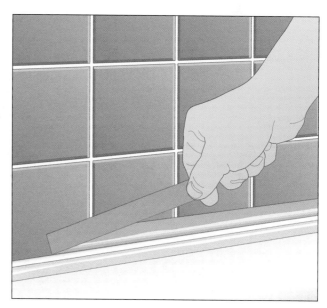

2 Pull the tape away
Pry up one end of a piece of tape and pull it away, taking care not to smear caulk on the tub. Do the same for the other piece of tape.

TILING AROUND A WINDOW

Windows located above bathtubs are notorious trouble spots. Painted wood trim usually cannot withstand a daily soaking, so rot develops. The solution is to remove the trim—the sill, the apron (the horizontal piece below the sill), and the jamb (which runs around the inside of the window's recess). Then cover the exposed areas with backerboard, and tile over it. If the window itself is rotting, install a vinyl replacement window or glass block. Where there is no other source of ventilation, however, you must still be able to open the window; a glass block installation must include a vent that can be opened.

Choose the Tiling Ensemble

The front portion of each side of the window recess should be tiled with bullnose tiles, which have sealed, rounded edges. You may be able to cover the sides of the recess with a single row of bullnose tiles, or you may need to install cut tiles behind them. Also consider installing a decorative border as part of the wall around the window.

Laying Out

Install a batten and set the tiles in a dry run on top (see page 123). Use a level to check that the cut tiles on either side of the window are the same size; adjust if necessary. If the window is not centered on the wall, centering the tiles on the window may mean that the cut tiles on either side of the wall are differently sized. Usually, the window is the more obvious focal point, so tiling symmetrically around it takes precedence.

Make a jury stick (see page 68), and use it to check the verti-

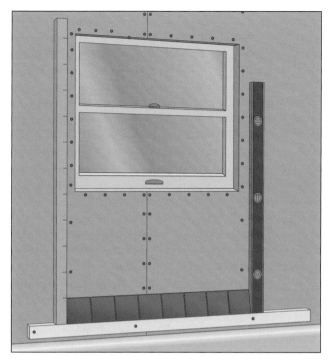

cal layout. Avoid ending up with a row of narrow tile slivers under the sill; if possible, these tiles should be at least half size. If you need to move the batten up or down, make sure the tiles in the bottom row—those that meet the tub—are also at least half size.

If you will be tiling above the window, check that those tiles also will not be slivers. You may want to make the tiles above the window the same size as those below the sill, but that is not as important.

Setting the Tiles

First, install all the wall tiles except the cut tiles around the window recess. Cut and install the partial wall tiles and the recess tiles at the same time, so you can make adjustments if necessary.

It's important that the cut tiles on the wall around the opening form straight lines. In most cases, the cut edges of those tiles should be on the same plane as the sides of the recess; the thickness of the mortar for the recess tiles will create the right grout line width. However, if your other grout lines are wider than usual, you may need to cut the wall tiles a little short, so they don't quite reach the recess. Experiment by

resting bullnose tiles on the sides of the recess where they will go. For a tile surface with normal width grout lines, the bullnose tiles should just rest against the cut edges of the wall tiles. The thickness of the mortar will produce a ⅛-inch grout spacing.

When tiling the recess, install the bullnose tiles on the sides first. Their front edges should just cover the unfinished edges of the wall tiles. Then cut and install the tiles behind them, if there are any. Next, install the recess tiles at the top. You may want to use organic mastic for these tiles, because thinset does not have as much hanging power before it sets.

When applying mortar for the sill tiles, mound it up towards the back so the tiles will be tilted slightly downward, allowing water to run off easily. Grout the tiles, and carefully caulk the inside corner where the tiles meet the window.

TILING A CEILING

Rarely does a ceiling need to be tiled for practical reasons; a good coat of enamel paint can protect ceiling surfaces from condensation produced by rising steam. But you may want the feel of total enclosure, whether in the tub area or even an entire room.

As long as you use organic mastic, actually setting the tiles in a ceiling is not difficult; press the tiles firmly into place, and they will not fall down. However, getting the layout right is difficult enough that you may want to consider hiring a pro for any ceiling tile job.

Whether you do the work or a professional does, install the ceiling tiles before the wall tiles if possible. It's easier to install wall tiles that cover up the cut ends of ceiling tiles than vice versa. Tiling a ceiling is also much easier if you use self-spacing tiles.

INSTALLING STRAIGHT-CUT CEILING TILES

If adjacent walls are square and straight, install ceiling tiles with grout lines parallel to the walls. Lay out both the walls and the ceiling before setting any tiles.

Laying out: Make the initial layout lines for the walls (see page 123). With the wall tiles placed in a dry run, use a level to draw additional vertical lines on the wall, spaced three or four tiles apart. Also draw lines showing where the cut tiles will go at the corners. Double-check all lines to make sure they are accurate and square. Use a straight edge and a pencil to draw a grid of layout lines on the ceiling based on the wall lines.

Installing the tiles: Install the wall tiles to within one or two tiles of the ceiling. Because things do not always turn out exactly as planned, you may need to make slight adjustments to the layout lines on the ceiling.

Once you are sure of your ceiling layout, use a notched trowel to spread organic mastic, taking care not to cover up the layout lines. Install the full-sized tiles first (including any bullnose tiles at the front edge of the installation, if only part of the ceiling is to be tiled), then measure and cut the ceiling tiles that abut the walls. Finally, install the remaining wall tiles.

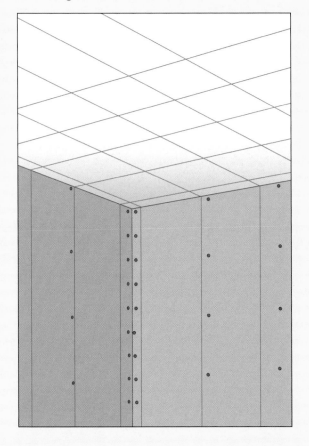

Assume that you will be installing full-sized triangles at one wall, and use the jury stick to find out the size of the cut tiles at all the walls. If necessary, adjust the layout to avoid tiny cut pieces.

Installing the tiles: Snap perpendicular layout lines near the center of the ceiling. Double-check the layout by using the jury stick to measure out from the layout lines. Use a notched trowel to spread organic mastic on the ceiling, and set the full-sized tiles. Then cut and install the corner pieces. This can be painstaking work, especially if the walls are wavy. After the tiles have set, apply grout as you would for a wall.

ANGLE-CUT TILES

If the ceiling area to be tiled is large, or if the walls are out of square (as they often are), installing parallel tiles can get very tricky. Matching the grout lines on one wall is not a problem, but matching the lines with two or three adjacent walls can drive you crazy.

One common solution is to install the ceiling tiles at a 45-degree angle to the walls. That way, the grout lines do not have to match up.

Laying out: Of course, it's impossible to do a dry run on a ceiling. So plan carefully to avoid ending up with tiny triangles at any of the walls. Check the ceiling for square, using the 3-4-5 method (see pages 66–67) as well as a framing square. Cut seven or eight tiles at 45-degree angles, lay them on the floor with spacers, if any, and make a jury stick (see page 68).

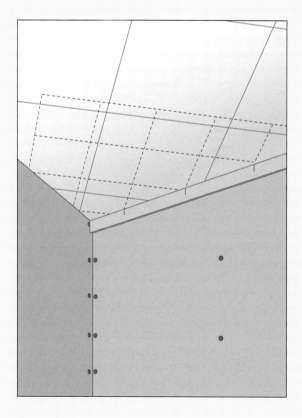

TILING A FIREPLACE SURROUND

A hearth and the area around a fireplace do not add up to much square footage, so you can choose expensive tiles without breaking your budget. Carefully arrange decorative tiles, like those on page 111, or install large stone tiles for a rough-hewn look, as shown in the following pages.

Install tiles for a fireplace project in latex-reinforced thinset mortar; organic mastic weakens when it is exposed to heat.

Hearth and Wall Options

In older homes, the hearth rests on a thick slab of concrete, which is supported by massive framing. Both the hearth and wall tiles are typically set in a thick mortar bed, making them very difficult to remove. If possible, find a way to tile on top of the existing tiles instead.

Often, a wood mantle surrounds the wall tiles on three sides, with trim pieces (usually, quarter-round or cove molding) covering the edges of the

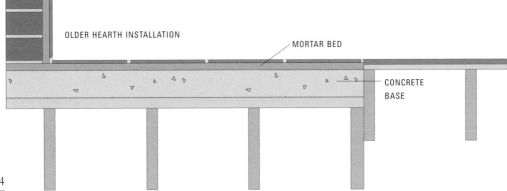

OLDER HEARTH INSTALLATION

MORTAR BED

CONCRETE BASE

tiles. You may be able to remove the trim pieces, install the new tiles, and put back the original trim. If not, either butt the tiles against the mantle precisely, or install new trim pieces to cover the edges of the tiles.

Some old hearths are too small, allowing sparks to fly out and damage the floor. In that case, if the tiles are flush with the height of the surrounding floor, you can lay cement backerboard on top of the tile and extend the backerboard over the nearby flooring. Attach the backerboard to the tiles with epoxy thinset, and to the flooring with screws. Install tiles on top of the backerboard. For a hearth that is too small, but raised, you may be able to use cement backerboard and wood framing to extend it.

Preparing the Surfaces and the Tiles

If the surfaces to be tiled are level and not glossy, they are ready for tiling. To tile over a rough surface like brick, check with a straightedge for high spots, and level them with a grinder. Then clean the surface with a mild solution of muriatic acid. For glazed tiles, go over the entire surface with a grinder to remove the glossy finish.

Mix a small batch of latex-reinforced thinset mortar. Use the flat side of a trowel to apply a thin "bond coat" of mortar to the surface. This fills in any grout lines and other irregularities.

Porous stone tiles must be sealed before they are installed, or the mortar will stain them permanently. Lay out the stones on a drop cloth and apply sealer with a brush or a rag to the top and sides of every tile. Plan to seal the tiles again after they have been installed (see page 137).

Installing Hearth Tiles and a Temporary Support

After the bond coat dries, apply thinset with a notched trowel and set the hearth tiles, using spacers to maintain consistent grout lines (see pages 74–75). Allow the mortar to set overnight.

If you are installing glazed tiles, you may want to use bullnose tiles around the edges of the firebox, depending on how finished a look you want to achieve. Some installations also include a row or two of tiles inside the firebox, running vertically along the sides and sometimes along the underside of the top as well.

Construct a 2-by-4 wooden frame as a temporary support for the first row of tiles above the firebox. Check that the tiles resting on it will be at exactly the correct height, and check that the support is level. Install the first tiles using the techniques shown on the following pages.

Setting the Wall Tiles

As with the hearth tiles, use latex-reinforced thinset mortar for the wall tiles around a fireplace. Use a large-notched trowel to apply the mortar, to ensure that the tiles are fully bedded. Make sure to purchase spacers so you can ensure consistent grout lines.

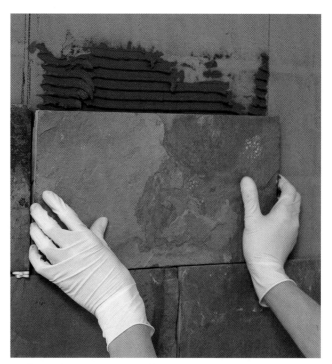

1 Place the tile
When installing large tiles like these, spread enough adhesive for only two or three tiles at a time. Back-butter each tile with a thin coat of mortar to ensure a firm bond. Place the tile on spacers for consistency.

2 Bed the tile
Press the tile firmly into place. If necessary, use a beater block to embed the tile firmly and to bring its surface flush with the surrounding tiles. To make sure a tile is properly bedded, pull it out and examine the back; there should be pulled-up mortar on nearly the entire surface.

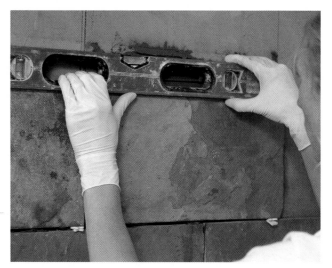

3 Check for level
Place a level on top of a tile or row of tiles to make sure you are staying level. Adjust with the spacers if necessary. Wipe away any mortar from the surface of the tile before moving on to the next tile.

Setting the Bullnose Pieces

Cut the bullnose trim pieces to fit. Lay out a dry run, so you know that all the tiles are cut correctly and ready to install. Where a trim piece rests on top of another tile, spread a thick layer of thinset, taking care not to drip on the new tile. Gently set the trim piece in place, and use spacers to position it precisely. Wipe away any excess mortar. Set the adjacent trim tiles quickly, so you can make any adjustments in all the pieces before the mortar starts to set.

Sealing Stone Tiles

Once the mortar has set, apply sealer to stone surface or porous tiles. Pay attention to the rate of absorption; some areas may be more porous than others, and will need an extra coat. Allow the sealer to dry for the recommended amount of time, and apply grout.

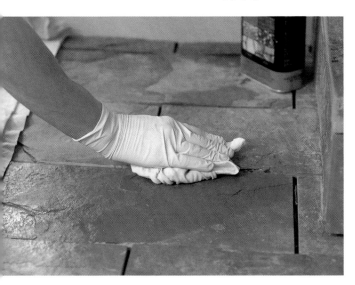

Wherever a tile edge is exposed, it should be finished with a bullnose edge. If bullnose pieces are not manufactured, you could hire professionals to make factory-like smooth finished edges. In the case of stone tiles, the edges do not have to be perfect, so you may choose to do it yourself using a grinder. Consult with your tile dealer to choose the grinding disks that will work best with your tile.

Place the tile on a stable surface; you may want to clamp it in place. Equip the grinder with the roughest recommended disk. (For these hard slate tiles, a diamond cutting blade was used.) Turn the grinder on and hold the disk at a 45-degree angle to the tile corner. Using gentle pressure, set the blade on the far side of the tile and pull it toward you. It will take four passes or so to create a slightly rounded edge.

Switch to a slightly less coarse disk (in this case, an extra-coarse marble-polishing disk), and repeat the process. Switch again to the smoothest disk (here, a coarse marble disk), and repeat.

TILING COUNTERTOPS

Though they have been common-place for years in the western and southwestern regions of the United States, tiled countertops are still viewed with suspicion by many. Isn't the surface too bumpy, and won't the grout lines become hopelessly stained?

In fact, a correctly tiled countertop is easy to keep clean, and requires only a small amount of additional maintenance. If you use epoxy grout, you won't even need to apply grout sealer.

Tiling a countertop allows you to choose from among a dazzling array of colors and styles. But take care that you get all the parts you need. A tile dealer should carry V-caps (opposite, bottom right) or other edge trim tiles, bullnose pieces, and borders specifically made for countertop use. Special corner pieces for the outside corners of the front edge are available as are pieces with bullnosed edges for the backsplash. If tiled countertops are not common in your area, you may need to special-order a tile ensemble. Make a scale drawing of your installation, and go over it in detail to make sure no little piece is missing.

A deep-blue bowl sink rests on a base of yellow glass tiles, surrounded by a countertop of complementary ceramic tiles. The lively mosaic trim tiles have a metallic finish.

Pink, green, and blue glossy ceramic tiles work surprisingly well together in this child's bathroom.

Natural stone tiles make an attractive countertop surface, but some types must be sealed regularly to protect against staining. Here, the front edge is finished with hardwood trim covered with several coats of high-gloss enamel paint.

Granite tiles that are 12 inches square are just the right size for a 24-inch-deep countertop. Narrow grout lines make it feel much like a granite slab.

Short radius bullnose pieces outline the curved top of a backsplash; the space below is filled with hand-broken shards of tile.

Instead of using raised art tiles only on a wall, this homeowner boldly chose them for the entire bathroom countertop and backsplash.

The soft peach hue of these handmade ceramic tiles makes a romantic statement in a bathroom designed for two. Accent tiles set at random among the field tiles add interest and appeal.

Tumbled marble tile, with its pitted surface and uneven edges, brings understated elegance to this informal kitchen. Rough stone tiles are in special need of regular sealing.

Carefully cut slate tiles fit around an underhung copper bathroom sink, with the tile edges polished for a smooth transition. Additional cut pieces circle the faucet handles on the backsplash.

SINK OPTIONS

If you're going to the trouble of putting in a new countertop, it probably makes sense to invest in a new sink as well. The plywood and backerboard making up a countertop substrate must be cut slightly differently for different types of sinks. Choose your sink and read the installation instructions before you install the substrate. Make sure that the base cabinet opening is large enough for the sink. For a kitchen installation, you will need a special "sink base," which has no drawers. Plan to install the sink near the center of the sink base, so it will not bump into the side of the cabinet.

Stainless-steel sinks come in a variety of price ranges; the more expensive models have a shinier surface that is easier to clean than that of less expensive models. If you buy a stainless-steel sink, make sure yours has sound-deadening insulation. Enameled steel and acrylic sinks are inexpensive, but not durable; spend a little more for an enameled cast-iron sink, which will stay attractive for decades.

A "self-rimming" sink is the easiest to install. Cut the opening and test to see that the hole is the correct size, then tile the countertop and place the sink in the hole (see page 153).

Although self-rimming sinks are simple to install, crumbs tend to collect along and under the rim; this is particularly true of stainless steel self-rimming sinks. For an alternative that is easier to clean, install a "flush-mounted" sink. Cut the hole in the plywood, install the sink, then put in backerboard up to the sink. Bullnose tiles can then be installed on top of the backerboard and overlapping the rim of the sink.

Or choose an "underhung" sink. This is the most difficult installation because of the number of cut tiles, but the result is attractive and easy to clean. Screw the sink to the underside of the plywood. Install narrow tile pieces along the vertical surface above the sink, and top off the edge where it meets the countertop with bullnose tiles.

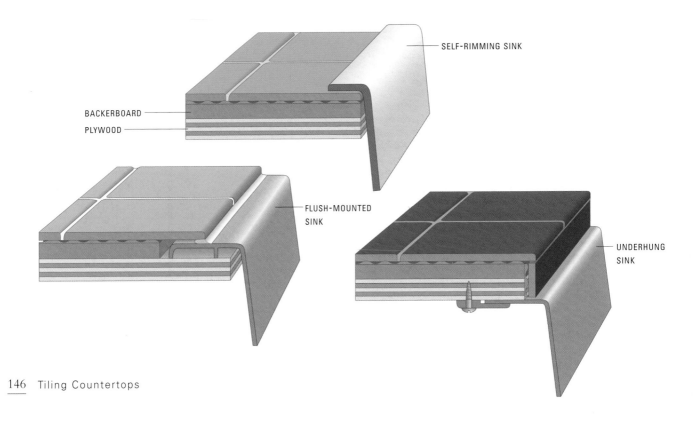

SELF-RIMMING SINK

BACKERBOARD

PLYWOOD

FLUSH-MOUNTED SINK

UNDERHUNG SINK

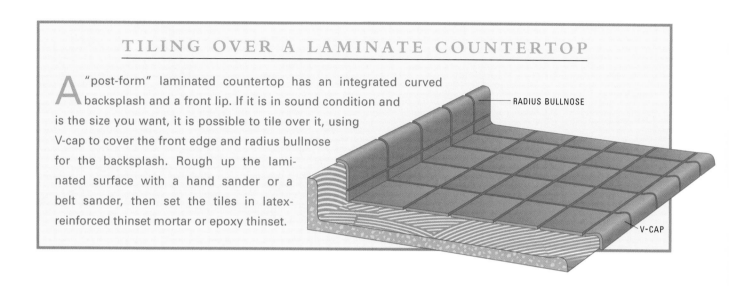

PREPARING THE SUBSTRATE

If you are installing new base cabinets, use shims both on the floor and against the wall to make the cabinets level in both directions. Attach the cabinets with screws driven through the back of the cabinets and into the wall studs. In the case of an existing countertop and cabinets, you may be able to tile over the old countertop (see above). If the existing countertop is tiled, it may be possible to pry off the tiles and scrape away the adhesive. For tiles set in mortar, pry away the substrate.

Removing a Sink

To take out the sink, first shut off water to the faucet and disconnect the supply lines. Disconnect the drain as well, and remove the garbage disposal if there is one.

If the sink is cast iron, slice through the caulking all around the underside of the lip of the sink, and pull up the sink. If the sink is stainless steel, it is probably clamped to the countertop with a series of clips underneath. Crawl underneath with a flashlight and screwdriver. Loosen the screws, and slide or turn the clips so they no longer hold. Then pull the sink out.

Removing a Countertop

Professionally installed countertops often have few fasteners—perhaps a screw driven up through the frame of the base cabinet every 4 feet or so. Use a flashlight to locate all the screws, and remove them. If construction adhesive or caulk has been applied to the underside of the countertop, slice through it with a utility knife. Pry the top gently with a flat prybar. If the top doesn't lift up easily, check again for fasteners; don't force it, or you may damage a base cabinet.

Building a New Substrate

Countertop tiles should rest on a surface that is solid and able to withstand moisture. The front edge must be thick enough to accommodate the edging you have chosen, and the substrate needs to be level in both directions.

In most cases, a layer of ¾-inch plywood topped with ½-inch or ¼-inch cement backerboard will do the job. A standard kitchen countertop is 25 inches deep; a backsplash is commonly 4 to 6 inches high. You can modify those dimensions in order to minimize cutting of tiles.

Before you begin work, protect the base cabinets from damage and falling mortar by covering them with plastic sheeting or construction paper. Also throw a drop cloth on the floor.

Two kinds of sinks are installed at this stage instead of after tiling. A flush-mounted sink is attached before the backerboard is in place, and an underhung sink just after the backerboard is installed.

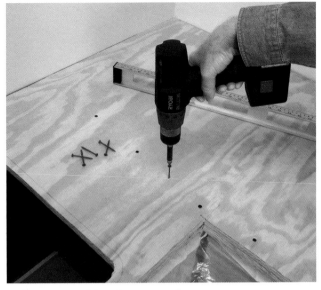

1 Install plywood

Purchase sheets of plywood that are free of warping, and store them stacked flat until you use them. Cut the pieces so that they overhang the cabinets by about an inch. To ensure that the front and side edges are straight and square, install with the factory edges (rather than the edges you have cut) facing out. Attach the plywood by driving 1⅝-inch deck screws (which resist rusting) through the plywood into the cabinet base every 6 inches or so. Check the entire surface to make sure it is level; if necessary, remove screws, install shims, and re-drive the screws. Cut a hole for the sink following the manufacturer's instructions. Lower the sink into the hole to make sure it fits. Attach a flush-mounted sink before adding the backerboard (see page 146).

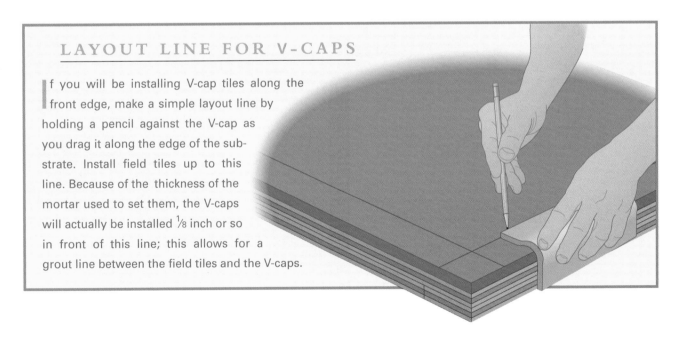

LAYOUT LINE FOR V-CAPS

If you will be installing V-cap tiles along the front edge, make a simple layout line by holding a pencil against the V-cap as you drag it along the edge of the substrate. Install field tiles up to this line. Because of the thickness of the mortar used to set them, the V-caps will actually be installed ⅛ inch or so in front of this line; this allows for a grout line between the field tiles and the V-caps.

2 Cut backerboard pieces to fit

See page 61 for instructions on how to cut backerboard. Size and arrange the pieces so that any seams in the backerboard are offset at least 3 inches from any seams in the plywood. Lay out the pieces in a dry run, and make sure the edges line up precisely with the plywood below, including the hole for a sink, if any. Test to make sure the sink will fit. For a flush-mounted sink, bring the backerboard up to the sink edge.

3 Set the backerboard in mortar

Mix a batch of latex-reinforced or epoxy thinset mortar. Spread thinset over the plywood using a ¼-inch notched trowel, only spreading enough for one backerboard piece each time. Lift up and install one piece of backerboard at a time. Lay the backerboard in the thinset, and drive 1¼-inch backerboard screws in a grid, spaced about 6 inches apart.

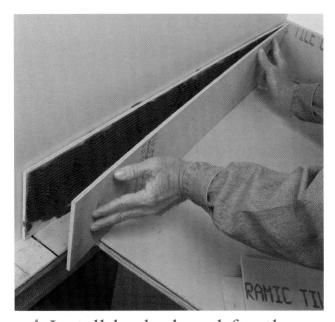

4 Install backerboard for the backsplash

If the backsplash will be tiled with radius bullnose or quarter-round trim at the top, cut pieces of backerboard to accommodate the thickness and width of the backsplash. Butter the back of the strips with thinset, and press them into place against the wall.

5 Tape the edges

Apply fiberglass mesh tape to the backerboard joints. Also wrap the front edges of the backerboard and plywood with the tape. Do not apply tape where the backsplash meets the countertop. Install an underhung sink before tiling (see page 146).

INSTALLING
THE TILES

Countertop tiles tend to be harder than wall tiles, which means that you may need to cut them with a wet saw. Many countertop tiles have rounded edges. When you cut a tile, however, the result is a sharp edge, which is easily damaged and more difficult to wipe clean. If possible, position all cut edges at the back of the countertop, where they will be covered by the backsplash tiles.

Laying Tiles in a Dry Run

Before you prepare the mortar, place the tiles on the substrate where they will go, with plastic spacers for the grout lines, and make adjustments as needed. Aim for a symmetrical look, with no narrow slivers of cut tiles.

For a countertop that turns a corner, start the layout at the inside corner. For a flush-mounted or

BATTEN POSSIBILITIES

To ensure that the first row of tiles is laid in a straight line, consider using a batten. It will probably save time in the long run.

For V-cap trim (above, right), rip-cut a strip of plywood and attach it temporarily with the factory edge (which is perfectly straight) along the layout line (see page 148).

For bullnose tiles (right), use a strip of wood that is the same thickness as the edging tile, plus ⅛ inch for the thickness of the mortar. Attach it to the face of the countertop, and install bullnose tiles that rest on the batten and come flush to its front edge.

For a wood edge trim (below, right), the field tiles should end exactly at the edge of the substrate. Attach a 1-by-2 board to the face of the substrate, and butt the tiles against it.

underhung sink (see page 146), you may want to start the layout at the sink, so you can have tiles of the same size on both sides of the sink.

If the layout ends up with a very narrow sliver, slightly widening the grout lines may solve the problem. Once you have planned the layout, mark and cut tiles as needed (see pages 70–71). In cutting the tiles, take into account the width of the grout lines on either side.

Making Special Cuts

Tiling a countertop may call for several complicated cuts. These can take a few attempts before you get them right, so have extra tiles on hand. If a tile must be cut at an angle as well as to length, make the angled cut first, hold the tile in place, and then make the length cut.

To cut two trim pieces for an inside corner (below), visualize how the cut should look, and roughly draw the direction of the cut on the tile. Position the tile on the tray of the cutter so the tile is oriented the same way as it will be installed. Cut both pieces longer than they need to be, so you can try again if necessary and not waste the tile. Test the pieces for fit, using spacers, and cut to length.

Make sure you understand how the pieces will all go together. Take into account the thickness of the mortar: Field tiles will be about ⅛ inch higher than they were in the dry run; edging and backsplash tiles will come forward about ⅛ inch.

INSTALLING
COUNTERTOP
TILES AT
AN ANGLE

The decorative look of diagonal tiles requires painstaking work, but is not difficult as long as you have a high-quality wet saw. Choose tiles with thick glazing, so you can round off the cut edges with a sanding block.

Practice cutting with a wet saw until you are sure you can make precise 45-degree cuts; you may need to slightly adjust the saw's sliding tray. Cut a number of tiles in half diagonally, at 45 degrees, and place them in a dry run along the layout line. Use as many full-sized tiles as possible, and make adjustments as needed to avoid small triangles.

Setting the Tiles

Leave the dry run in place. To be sure that you can follow the layout, remove only a few linear feet of tiles at a time, set them in mortar, and then do the same for the next few linear feet of tiles. In most cases, you should install the field tiles first, then the edging and the backsplash.

1 Apply the thinset

Mix as much latex-reinforced or epoxy thinset mortar (see page 73) as you can use in half an hour or so. If the mortar starts to harden while you are working, throw it out and mix a new batch. Spread the mortar onto the backerboard using a ¼-inch square-notched trowel. To ensure a flat surface for the tiles, hold the trowel at the same angle the entire time, and scrape away any globs of thinset.

2 Set the field tiles

Starting at the layout lines or the batten, press the full-sized and cut tiles into the mortar. Position plastic spacers to keep all the grout lines the same width. Use a straightedge to make sure the lines are straight, and tap the tiles into the mortar using a beater block (see page 74).

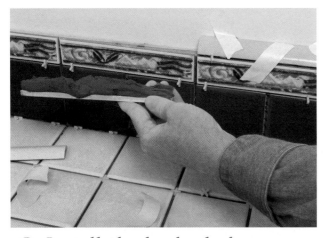

3 Install the backsplash

Back-butter the backsplash tiles, or comb mortar onto the backerboard strip with the trowel. Use spacers to hold the bottom backsplash piece the width of a grout line above the field tiles. If there is a small quarter-round piece at the top (as shown), fill in the space above the backerboard strip with plenty of mortar, so the quarter-round can nest in it. If necessary, use strips of masking tape to hold the pieces together while they set.

4 Set the edging

Either back-butter the edging tiles with mortar, or apply mortar to the edge. Some types of edging, such as V-cap, can be simply set in the mortar because they rest on the horizontal surface of the substrate. If the edging attaches primarily to the vertical substrate edge, use masking tape to hold the tiles in place until the mortar sets. Use spacers to position the edging pieces, and hold them firmly in place while you apply the tape. Every few minutes, check that the edging pieces haven't moved down; you may need to reapply the tape.

Finishing

Allow the mortar to harden overnight. Use a laminated grout float to push grout into the gaps between the tiles and then squeegee away the excess. Wipe the surface and tool the grout lines with a sponge, then buff the surface with a dry cloth (see page 77).

Use a utility knife to cut away the grout along the bottom of the backsplash, and apply a bead of caulk to this joint (see pages 117 and 129 for two caulking methods).

Install a self-rimming sink according to the manufacturer's instructions. To put in a cast-iron sink, place a bead of silicone caulk all around the hole, set the sink in it, and wipe away the excess. For a stainless-steel sink, apply plumber's putty to the underside of the sink, and clamp the sink to the countertop using the clips provided by the manufacturer.

Save time and hassles by hooking most of the plumbing—the faucet, drain, and garbage disposer—onto the sink before setting the sink in the hole.

TILING A BACKSPLASH WALL

The word "backsplash" can refer to a strip of tile or wood about 4 inches wide attached to the wall at the rear of the countertop (see page 152). Or, it may refer to tiling on the wall behind the countertop—usually, the vertical space between the countertop and the wall cabinets, or between the range and the range hood. This space is typically about 18 inches high.

In general, backsplash tiles are installed like other wall tiles (see pages 112–117). The substrate does not have to be waterproof or particularly strong; you can simply tile over any wall surface that is in sound condition. Any type of ceramic or stone tile can be used, as long as it is easily washable. Organic mastic will be strong enough, but you can use thinset mortar if you expect the surface to get wet often.

If backsplash tiles butt into a wall cabinet, simply run the field tiles to about $\frac{1}{8}$ inch below the cabinet. Wherever the top edge of the tiles will be exposed, however, use bullnose trim pieces for a finished look. Where backsplash tiles meet the countertop below or a cabinet above, fill the joint with caulk rather than grout to prevent cracking.

You'll probably need to cut tiles to fit around several electrical outlets or switches (see page 105). If the new tile recesses an electrical box more than $\frac{1}{4}$ inch from the wall surface, install a box extender (see page 117). You may also need to purchase extra-long screws to re-attach the outlet or switch.

TILING OUTDOORS

Tile or stone adds a personal touch to patios, walkways, porches, and pool surrounds. With tile, you can decorate the outdoors not only with natural earth tones, but also with splashes of color.

Sturdy patios can be made by setting concrete pavers or bricks in sand. This chapter, however, concentrates on true tiling—setting tiles or stones in a bed of mortar on top of a solid concrete slab.

Exterior tiles have long been common in areas with warm climates. In colder areas, where tile installations can buckle or crack during the winter, exterior tiles have been less common. However, new manufacturing techniques produce tiles that hold up under severe freezing conditions. And if you use mortar and grout that are rated stable for freezing and thawing, the installation ought to survive even the most severe winter.

Choose tiles with a proven record in your area, and with a non-slip surface. In areas with freezing winters, buy tiles that are vitreous or impervious. In warmer areas, almost any tile—even a soft saltillo—will stay strong as long as it is completely embedded in mortar.

Fossilized flagstone—
both in tile form and in
jagged shapes—runs
through the living room
and onto the patio,
blurring the distinction
between indoors and out.

Bands of African slate run through a patio of saltillo tiles. Criss-crossing the slate are 3-inch-wide gaps that allow for lush plantings.

Marble can be used as an outdoor surface if it is mortared onto a solid concrete slab. The curved cuts necessary for this type of installation can be made by pros with special equipment.

Unsealed saltillo tiles will soak up the water, making for a pleasant place to dry off after a swim. Moisture-resistant glazed ceramic tiles are used for the pool surround.

Variegated marble-like hues in these Indian slate tiles brighten in the sun to create a sumptuous poolside patio.

A staircase of cut flagstones spruced up with colorful ceramic tiles on the risers beckons visitors onto the patio of this Mediterranean-style home.

Terra-cotta tiles are set at regular intervals in this concrete slab, which was tinted when it was poured. A similar effect can be achieved by applying stain to an existing slab.

A flagstone patio in desert hues blends in well with the landscape. Rough-edged stone tiles cover the stairs leading to the house.

This intricate ceramic tile border is positioned to reflect in the water below.

Sealed terra-cotta tiles climb up a long flight of stairs in this hillside garden.

At this desert home, 12-by-12 limestone tiles wrap around a curved pool. The natural stone stays cool underfoot—a welcome feature during the summer months.

The muted colors of slate tiles add texture and warmth to the terrace and fireplace of a cozy outdoor room.

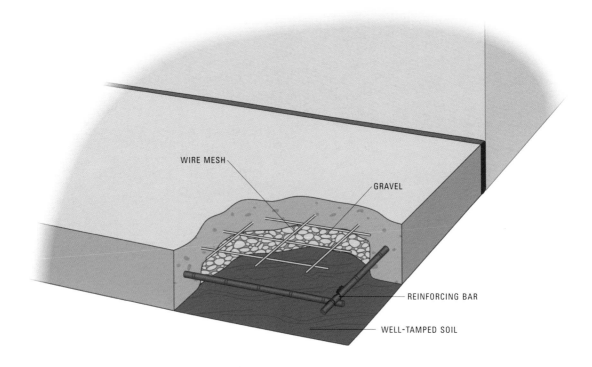

WIRE MESH

GRAVEL

REINFORCING BAR

WELL-TAMPED SOIL

PREPARING A CONCRETE SLAB FOR TILING

For best results, tile should be installed on a concrete slab that is strong, fairly flat, and correctly sloped. If you do not already have a slab, consult with a contractor or check a masonry book.

A Slab that is Strong Enough

New tile and mortar add only a small amount of strength, so check that the slab is in sound condition before you tile over it. If possible, find out how well it was built. A slab should be at least 3 inches thick, and preferably reinforced with wire mesh or reinforcing bars. It should rest on a bed of gravel, which in turn rests on solid soil. The periphery of the slab should be deeper and may or may not rest on a gravel bed. Unfortunately, you may not be able to obtain this information, since all you can see is the top of the concrete.

Still, you can learn much about a slab by examining it. Many problems are cosmetic rather than structural.

Ugly stains and discoloration are not a problem. Cracks that are less than ½ inch wide are reparable. Small protrusions can be ground down, and small holes can be filled.

Other problems are more serious. If the slab is cracked and buckled, so that part of it is at a slant, or if one section rises above the other by more than ½ inch, the slab is not stable. Of course, no part of the slab should wobble when you walk on it. If a large area of the surface is flaking off, or has a pattern of closely spaced cracks, tiles installed over it may come loose in time. Consult with a concrete contractor if you are at all unsure.

A patio slab should also slope down and away from the house at a rate of about ¼ inch per foot, to avoid standing water. If puddles form on the slab after a rainfall, the same thing will happen after you tile over it. In areas with freezing winters, this can cause tiles to crack when the puddles freeze.

Patching Cracks and Holes

Before tiling, repair the surface so it is firm and flat; don't count on the tile mortar to fill any depressions deeper than ½ inch.

To repair a crack or a small hole, chip away any loose pieces using a cold chisel and a small sledge hammer. Wear protective eye gear as you work. Widen cracks to at least 1 inch. "Key" holes and cracks, so that the bottom is wider than the top. Flush out all dust and debris with water from a hose. Allow the slab to dry, and apply concrete bonding agent to any holes (see page 170). Mix a batch of concrete patch (work quickly if it is fast-setting) and trowel it over holes and cracks. Scrape the area fairly smooth so there are no protrusions.

For an extra measure of protection against cracking, you may choose to apply an isolation membrane to the concrete surface (see pages 64–65).

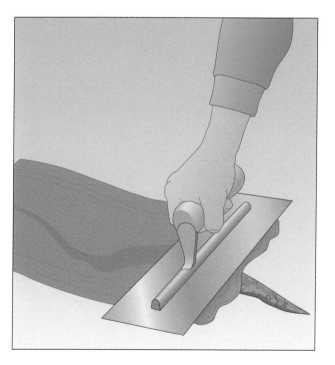

Adding an Expansion Joint

Where the slab meets the house, or any other vertical structure, there should be a gap that is filled with flexible material to allow for expansion in extreme weather. This can be a fibrous material made for the purpose, or you can fill the gap with a thick bead of caulk.

LAYING A SALTILLO TILE PATIO

Mexican tiles called saltillos are popular in the West and Southwest, where winters are warm. Because the tiles are soft, they cannot survive a freezing winter. They are also hand-made, so they vary significantly in size and shape, and are often severely curved. You can also follow these instructions when installing any irregularly shaped tile. (To lay more regular factory-made tiles on an outdoor surface, follow the instructions for floor tiles given on pages 62–77.)

Before any tile installation, wash the concrete slab clean of all oils and debris using a mild solution of muriatic acid or a strong solution of TSP. Rinse the surface thoroughly, and allow it to dry. You may choose to apply concrete bonding agent as well (see page 170).

Laying Out with Grid Lines

Often, saltillos and other large exterior tiles are laid in 3-foot-square sections, each of which holds nine tiles. Test that this arrangement will lead to grout lines of the width that you want. (On an exterior installation, wide grout lines are the norm.) Lay three tiles next to each other on a flat surface, spaced as you would like them to be in the finished installation. Measure the width of the three tiles, and add the width of one grout line; this is the size of the squares in which the tiles should be laid. Readjust as needed until you are satisfied.

Measure for the grid lines: Check the slab to make sure it is square (see page 66). If the slab is out of square, draw square lines and make all your measurements from the lines, not from the edges of the slab. Measure the length and width of the installation, and divide by the chosen width of the sections (as described above). You may want to plan so the cut tiles are the same size at either end, although this is not critical in an outdoor installation. In both directions along the slab, make a V-shaped mark every

3 feet, or at every multiple of the chosen width for the squares.

Snap lines: Snap one chalk line going in either direction, and check the resulting corner to make sure it is square; make adjustments in the marks if necessary. Snap all the lines, to produce a grid of squares on the entire surface to be tiled.

Applying the Mortar

Purchase medium-bed thinset mortar, which holds its shape when laid on thick. If that is not available, combine regular thinset mortar with an equal amount of brick and block mortar. For a small job, mix the mortar in a bucket using a mixing paddle (see page 73). If the patio is more than 100 square feet, you may want to mix larger amounts in a wheelbarrow (see page 171). The mortar should be just stiff enough to cling to a trowel held vertically for a second or two.

To apply the mortar, use a trowel with large notches—at least ⅜ by ¼ inch. Depending on the tiles, you may need a trowel with large, scallop-shaped notches; consult with your tile dealer to choose the best one. A trowel that is 16 inches long makes it easier to keep the mortar level.

Spread the mortar: Using the flat side of a trowel, spread a thick coat—about 1 inch—inside one of the squares. Take care not to cover the working lines. Spread with long, sweeping strokes to produce a surface that is fairly level.

Trowel the mortar: With the notched side of a trowel, comb the surface of the mortar only; the notches should not scrape the concrete. Work to create an even surface with no globs or gaps.

Setting the Tiles

The saltillos shown here are reasonably smooth and flat. Others are so rough that you need to scrape the backs before installing them. If a saltillo is particularly curved, back-butter the concave portion before setting it in the mortar. The saltillos used in this project are covered with a clear glaze. If yours are unglazed, apply sealer both before and after installing. If the tiles are installed without having been sealed, the mortar and grout will stain the tiles.

The mortar must be wet enough to stick to the tiles, but stiff enough to hold up the tile. If mortar flows out from under the sides of the tiles, stiffen the mix by adding dry ingredients. If the mortar has started to set and will not adhere to the tiles, throw it out and make a new batch.

Place and align the tiles: Each square holds nine tiles. Position the upper left tile so that two of its edges align with the layout lines. The two tiles to the right should align with the top line, and the two tiles below should align with the left line. Place the center tile next. On the right and bottom sides of the square, however, the tiles should be one grout line short of the layout lines. Stand up and examine the nine tiles from several angles. The grout lines will not be perfect, but they should be as close to straight and consistent in width as possible. Move on to the next square only when you are completely satisfied.

Bed the tiles and check adhesion: Gently tap the tiles with a hammer over a block of wood to embed them in the mortar and create a smooth tile surface. In every square, pick up at least one tile to make sure the mortar is sticking to three-quarters or more of the back surface. If not, back-butter the tiles.

When the spaces between tiles are wide and the tiles are uneven, grouting gets messy. Work the grout in between the tiles by pushing with a grout float in at least two directions at all points. Squeegee away as much of the excess grout as you can. Drag a wet towel over the area, then wipe lightly with a damp sponge. You will need to rinse the sponge often. Once the grout starts to stiffen, use the sponge to create grout lines that are consistent in depth. Allow the grout to harden, then buff the surface with a dry cloth.

Cutting Saltillos and Other Soft Tiles

Soft tiles like saltillos are too uneven and too thick to cut with a snap cutter. Rent a wet saw if you have more than ten tiles to cut. To cut just a few tiles, clamp a wood guide on the tile and cut with a grinder equipped with a masonry or diamond blade (above). It will take several passes to cut about halfway through the tile; you can then snap it to finish the cut.

Grouting Large Joints

Check that the mortar has hardened all the way through before grouting. Because the mortar is so thick, this may take 2 days. Purchase sanded grout that is latex-reinforced. See pages 76–77 for general grouting instructions. Mix grout that is fairly stiff—just to the point where it does not pour readily.

SETTING FLAGSTONES

The term "flagstone" is a general designation for any stone that is generally flat but bumpy, with uncut edges. Also called "cleft" stones, flagstones can be set in sand or directly on top of tamped soil. For the firmest installation, however, lay them in a mortar bed on top of a concrete slab.

Flagstones vary from 1 to 3 inches in thickness. Save money and lessen back strain by choosing the thinnest possible stones. Even with thinner stones, it's a good idea to enlist some helpers and take plenty of breaks.

At a stone or landscaping supply source, you can purchase for delivery a pallet of stones that weighs from 1 to 2 tons. Most pallets contain stones of varying thickness. Colors include gray, brown, and rust red. Some suppliers allow you to choose individual stones and load them onto your truck or van. (They weigh the vehicle before and after loading, and charge for the difference.) The supplier should be able to give you a general idea of how many square feet are covered by a ton of each type of stone.

Consult with your stone dealer to choose the best mortar for your type of stone. You may use a combination of thinset and brick mortar, or simply mix sand and Portland cement.

Apply Bonding Agent

Scrub the concrete surface with TSP or a mild muriatic acid solution, and rinse it thoroughly. To make certain that the mortar will stick to the concrete, brush liquid concrete bonding agent over the slab (left). Follow the manufacturer's directions; usually, you need to wait for the bonding agent to dry partially, and then apply mortar within a few hours.

Sort and Lay Out Stones

Make three or four piles of stones, arranged according to size. When you lay the stones out, choose some from each pile, so you end up with an even distribution of large, medium, and small stones.

Choose some of the largest and thickest stones, and scatter them throughout the slab, spaced 3 or 4 feet apart. This will ensure that you have large stones in all parts of the patio.

Mix the Mortar

A simple, strong, and inexpensive mortar can be made by mixing 3 parts sand with 1 part Portland cement. You can also add liquid latex to the mortar.

Place 6 shovelfuls of sand and 2 shovelfuls of Portland cement into a wheelbarrow, and mix them together with the shovel or a hoe. Gradually add water and continue to stir, scraping the bottom of the wheelbarrow to get up all the dry ingredients. The mortar must be stiff enough to hold up a stone, yet wet enough to stick. It should cling to a shovel held vertically for a second or two.

Set a Large Stone

Shovel enough mortar for a large stone onto the concrete, then partially smooth it using a mason's trowel. Set a large, thick stone in the mortar. Check that it is fairly level in both directions.

Lay Out a Dry Run

Fill in a 4-foot-square area around the large stone with dry-laid stones. Allow the stones to overhang the slab by as much as 2 inches, for a natural appearance. Aim for grout lines that are roughly uniform in width. You will find yourself shuffling, rearranging, and reorienting stones. Work with helpers and rest often to avoid hurting your back.

From time to time, you will need to cut a stone in order to make the jigsaw puzzle fit. Hold the stone in place, and draw a cut line.

Cut the Stones

If you follow the technique shown at right, the stone will break the way you want it to about 60 percent of the time; the rest of the time, it will choose its own course. If so, grab another stone and try again.

Wear protective eye gear because shards of stone will fly. Move the stone to an area where you can easily sweep away the shards. Using a cold chisel and a small sledge hammer, tap along the cut line to produce a series of small indentations. With the tip of the chisel on one of the score marks, strike the chisel with a sharp blow. If the stone does not break, move the chisel to another part of the cut and try again.

Spread the Mortar

Every 10 minutes or so, use a shovel or hoe to remix the mortar. If it starts to stiffen, add a little more liquid. If it stays stiff, throw it out and make a new batch.

Pick up one of the dry-laid stones and set it to the side, oriented so you can easily replace it in the correct position. Shovel some mortar onto the concrete, and use a trowel to roughly even it out. If the stone to be laid is thin, apply a thicker layer of mortar. With practice and plenty of trial and error, you can produce a stone surface that is reasonably level.

Set the Stones

Set the stones in mortar one at a time, and check that each is close to level and about the same height as its neighbor. Every few stones, use a straight board to check the height of the stones. Make any needed adjustments right away, before the mortar starts to set. If a stone is low, remove it, apply more mortar, and reset it. If a stone is too high, tap it down and scrape away the excess mortar that oozes out.

Fill Between the Stones

If you want to fill in between the stones with mortar, slip mortar into the gaps using a mason's trowel. Work carefully, to get as little mortar on the surface of the stones as possible. Use a small piece of wood or a striking tool to provide an even fill. Allow an hour or two for the mortar to dry partially, then sweep the surface lightly with a broom. Once the mortar is dry, spray the installation with water and clean the stones with a brush. If the stones are discolored by spilled mortar, wait a day and then clean the surface with a solution of muriatic acid.

For a more natural look, fill the joints with fine, crushed stone (below). This will become fairly hard, but it will permit a small amount of water to seep in; consult with your stone dealer to determine whether it is safe to use it in your area. After the mortar under the flagstones has set, pour some crushed stone onto the surface. Sweep the stones in several directions, to work it in deeply between the flagstones. You may need to pick up some larger stones if they get caught in a narrow space. Using a garden hose with the nozzle set on "mist," spray the entire surface (below). This will cause the finer particles to settle downward. Allow the surface to dry, sweep more crushed stone into the cracks, and spray again. Repeat until the filler stones are nearly flush with the surface of the stones.

TILING STAIRS

Y ou can dress up plain concrete or wood steps by covering them with tile. One option is to install accent tiles over part or all of the risers; another is to cover the entire surface.

Tiling Risers on Wood Stairs

Tiling over wooden stair treads is risky, because most treads flex slightly when they are walked on. Consider installing tile on the risers only, where they can contrast attractively with wood-toned or painted treads.

The treads should overhang the existing risers by an inch or so, to cover the thickness of the backerboard and the tiles. If they do not overhang sufficiently, you may be able to remove the fasteners and adjust the tread positions.

Use radius bullnose pieces to cover the edges of the backerboard on the sides. Purchase large tiles that are as tall as the risers, or plan to install two horizontal rows of tiles.

Cut a strip of concrete backerboard ½ inch shorter than the riser. Attach it to the riser with screws, leaving a ¼-inch gap at the top and the bottom. Cut and install tiles so there is a ⅛-inch gap at the bottom and top. Fill these gaps with caulk rather than grout, so the tiles won't crack when the treads flex.

Tiling over Concrete Steps

If concrete steps have chipped edges, repair them using patching concrete. Grind down any high spots, so the tiles can be laid evenly. If a tile sticks up a little higher than its neighbor, it can be easily chipped, and may present a tripping hazard.

Purchase durable vitreous or impervious tiles with a non-skid surface. You'll need radius bullnose pieces for the front edge, and in some cases cove pieces for where a tread meets a riser. Apply concrete bonding agent to the stairs (see page 170), and set the tiles in latex-reinforced thinset mortar.

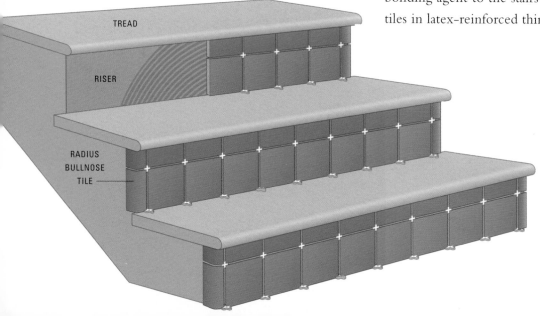

TREAD

RISER

RADIUS BULLNOSE TILE

HAND-CRAFTED STEPPING-STONES

If you have a yen to make hand-crafted features for a patio floor, this project allows plenty of scope for creativity. Broken tiles or shards from once-favorite dishes or vases can be reincarnated as parts of stepping-stones that are both beautiful and personal.

These stepping-stones can be set in mortar on a concrete slab, or laid in a bed of sand or well-tamped soil. Surround them with other pavers, or with loose material such as crushed granite or mulch.

For each stepping-stone, start with a ready-made concrete paver that was purchased at a home or garden center. If possible, buy pavers with smooth surfaces. Purchase latex bonding agent, latex-reinforced thinset mortar, and sanded grout as well.

Place the tile or pottery piece in a heavy-duty, self-sealing plastic bag, squeeze out most of the air, and close the bag. Wearing protective eyewear and gloves, tap the bag with a hammer to produce shards of the size you want. Expect to lose as much as one third of the material, because many pieces will be too small to use.

Trace the outline of your paver onto a piece of plywood. Arrange the shards until you are satisfied with the pattern; aim at grout lines that are fairly consistent. If the stepping-stone will have decorative elements, like the stars shown here, draw them on the paver.

Paint the paver with latex bonding agent, and allow it to dry partially. With a notched trowel, mix and apply thinset mortar to between one quarter and one half of the paver. Transfer the shards to the paver, pushing each shard into the mortar so it sticks. Lay mortar and set shards in another section of the paver, and continue until the stepping-stone is complete. Use a beater board to achieve a fairly level surface. Allow the mortar to set overnight or longer, and apply grout. After the grout is cured, apply outdoor grout sealer for extra protection.

CARE & REPAIR

Properly installed, most wall and floor tile will last for many decades with a minimum of care. However, porous ceramic and stone tile should be sealed regularly, or it will be vulnerable to staining. If you are not certain how to maintain your type of tile, see pages 6–31 or consult the chart on pages 186–188.

When damage is caused by a specific event, such as dropping a heavy object onto floor tile, it makes sense simply to repair the damaged section. If tiles develop cracks or come loose even when nothing unusual has happened, they were installed incorrectly. Wall tiles may have been used on a floor or countertop, the substrate may not be firm enough, or the wrong adhesive may have been used. In those cases, the solution is usually to remove all of the tiles and start over again.

Most problems with tiled surfaces arise not because of damage to the tiles themselves, but because the grout or caulk fails. Once gaps develop, moisture can sneak behind the tiles, where it may weaken the adhesive and damage the substrate or even the house's structure. This chapter shows how to clean and replace grout. For instructions on how to apply grout, see pages 117 and 129.

If it will be difficult to replace a damaged wall tile, consider painting it. Take a tile to a paint dealer, who should be able to produce oil-based gloss paint that nearly matches the color. Dull the tile's finish by rubbing it with fine sandpaper, then paint the tile with alcohol-based primer (also known as white shellac), which bonds firmly with glossy surfaces. Then apply two coats of finish paint. The resulting surface will stand up to cleaning and scrubbing as long as you do not use an abrasive cleaner.

REPLACING TILE

If more than one or two tiles are broken, look for an underlying problem. Jump on a floor or push on a wall with the heel of your hand. If you feel any flex, the substrate needs to be shored up; see pages 54–55 for some suggestions.

Should tiles come loose, remove them and check the substrate for damage. If you find damaged floor plywood or wall substrate, remove as many tiles as necessary to repair the substrate and perhaps even the framing. Install a patch of new cement backerboard before reinstalling the tiles.

Finding Replacement Tiles and Grout

Removing and replacing a tile is usually not a difficult task in itself; the hardest part may be finding a new tile and grout in colors that match. One manufacturer's teal tile will be subtly different from another's; the difference will be painfully apparent when the tile is installed. Even "white" tiles actually come in many different hues.

If the manufacturer's name is printed on the back of the damaged tile, you can do most of your looking by calling suppliers. If not, you'll have to drive to tile dealers with the old tile until you find one that matches.

Grout can be even more difficult to match. Even if you get the correct brand and color, chances are that your grout has slightly darkened after years of use. Clean the existing grout using grout cleaner. Chip off a piece of the cleaned grout and take it to a tile dealer. Look for the grout sample that comes closest to matching.

Replacing Floor Tile

When a floor tile has been properly set in thinset mortar, you must crack it into small pieces for removal. If a whole tile pops out, then the thinset is not strong enough; you may need to reinstall some surrounding tiles, and perhaps even the entire floor. Where the substrate is plywood, you may need to remove all of the tiles and the plywood, and install cement backerboard before retiling. Jump on the floor at a number of points. If you see or feel the floor flexing, see pages 54–55 for ways to strengthen a floor.

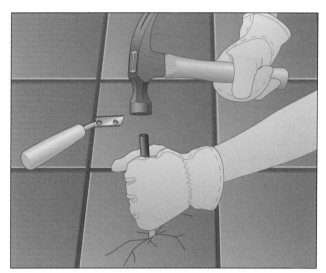

1 Chip out a damaged tile

All around the damaged tile, scrape out the grout using a grout saw (shown above). With a hammer and cold chisel, strike the center of the tile until it cracks. Pry out the tile shards.

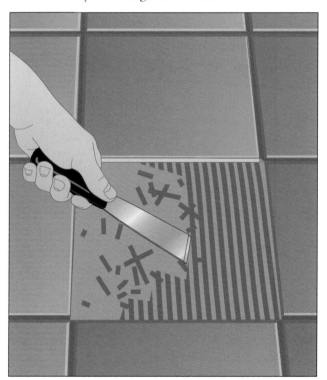

2 Scrape away the mortar

Use a putty knife or margin trowel (see page 38) to pry and then scrape out all the mortar and any remaining grout from the area. Vacuum away the dust, and rub with a damp cloth.

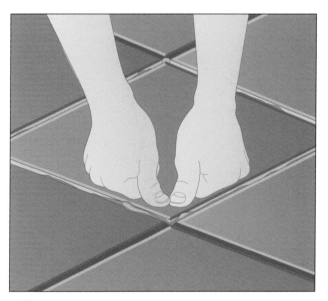

3 Set the new tile

Back-butter the tile (see page 75) and press it into place. Check that it is at the same level as the surrounding tiles, and wipe away any mortar that oozes out along the sides. Make sure all the grout lines are the same width. Allow the mortar to set overnight, then grout around the new tile.

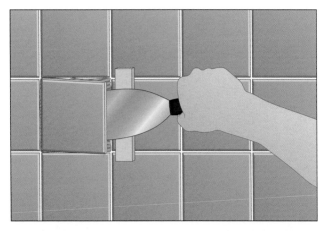

Replacing a Wall Tile

If a wall tile was installed using organic mastic, you probably can remove the entire tile. The tile may simply pull loose from the mastic, or the mastic and part of the wall may come along with it. If the paper covering of drywall or greenboard tears off, the wall will be weakened; replace the substrate if a large area of paper is missing.

Use a grout saw to remove the grout all around the tile. Keep sawing until you have reached the underlying wall. Insert a scraper or putty knife behind the tile, place a small piece of wood on the adjacent tile to protect it, and pry the damaged tile out. If the tile does not come out whole, break it and pull out the shards (see page 179).

Back-butter the replacement tile, press it into place, and wipe away the excess mastic. To make sure the tile does not slide down while the mastic is setting, use nails as spacers at the bottom and secure the tile in position with masking tape.

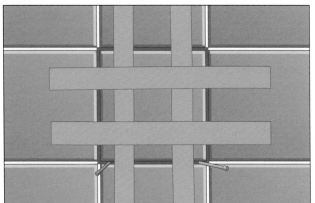

Replacing Resilient Floor Tile

If you cannot find an exact replacement for a damaged resilient tile, remove a tile from under the refrigerator or some other inconspicuous place.

If the damaged tile has started to curl up, or if there is a crack in it, slip in a putty knife and pry up the tile. If there is no easy point of entry, or the tile is difficult to remove, heat it with a clothes iron (set on high) to soften the mastic, keeping a cloth between the iron and the tile to avoid dirtying the face of the iron. Keep the iron moving, and stop if you smell burning. Once loosened, pry up with a putty knife.

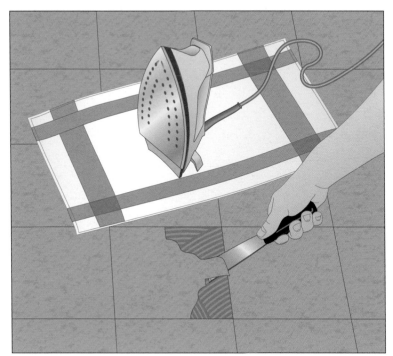

Scrape the area absolutely clean, and vacuum away all dust; even a small particle will show through most resilient tiles. Test to make sure the new tile will fit. Apply mastic to the floor, allow it to dry, and set the tile. Use a kitchen rolling pin to press the tile firmly into the mastic (right).

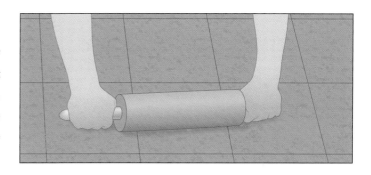

Replacing a Wood Parquet Tile

If part of a parquet tile is damaged, it's usually easier to replace the whole tile, rather than replacing one or two of the component strips. See pages 86–89 for instructions on installing wood parquet tiles.

The tile may have changed color over the years. To find a correct replacement, try to match a tile that has been hidden under the refrigerator or a cabinet.

Set the blade of a circular saw to cut just through the thickness of the parquet tile. Make several cuts across the tile; take care not to cut an adjacent tile. Now you can pry the tile out piece by piece (below). Scrape away all the adhesive from the floor.

Before installing a replacement tile, you must cut away the bottom portion of its groove on two sides, as well as one of the tongues (below). Set the circular saw for a very shallow cut, and remove the sections with the tile upside-down. Lay the new tile in place without adhesive to make sure it will fit. Apply parquet tile adhesive to the floor using a notched trowel, or use a caulking gun to squirt squiggles of construction adhesive that is labeled "for floors." Slip the tile into place, press down until its top is flush with the adjacent tiles, and wipe away any excess adhesive that oozes out. Place a heavy weight on the tile and leave it there for a day or so.

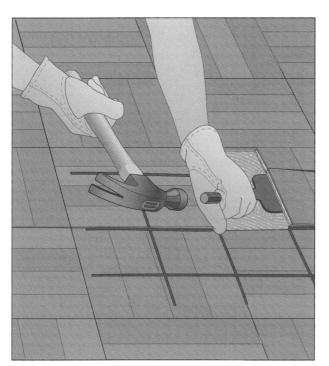

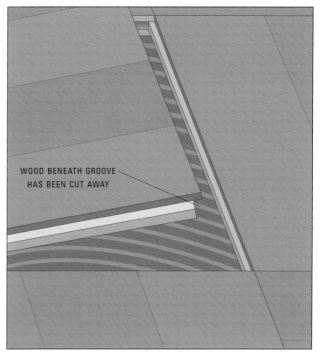

WOOD BENEATH GROOVE
HAS BEEN CUT AWAY

REPAIRS TO GROUT

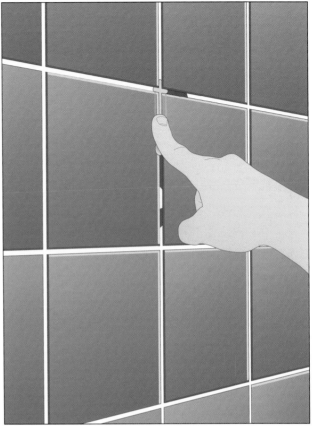

Often a tiled surface that looks old and dingy can be made attractive and new-looking simply by refurbishing the grout. If only a few holes are present, chances are the grout is strong but the installer missed a few spots, so patching makes sense. If grout is coming loose generally, it probably is not latex-reinforced; the grout should all be removed and the area regrouted. If the grout is stained in spots or is a dirty color, try cleaning it (see page 184).

Patching Holes in Grout

If you see even a small hole in the grout, patch it right away, before moisture has a chance to work its way behind the tiles. Mix a small batch of latex-reinforced grout (use sanded grout for grout lines ⅛ inch and wider, and unsanded grout for narrower grout lines). Press it in with your finger. Wipe away the excess, allow it to dry, and clean the area with a wet sponge.

Regrouting

If grout is recessed, applying a thin coat of grout on top is risky; there's a good chance that the new grout will flake off eventually. It's safest to take out all the grout with a grout saw before regrouting.

Removing grout from a wall or floor is painstaking work, but well worth the effort. Saw with slow, deliberate strokes to avoid damaging any tiles. Apply only moderate pressure; let the grout saw do most of the work. If the going starts to get slow, the saw may have become dull; buy another one. If you have a lot of grout to remove, consider buying an electric grout-removal tool.

Vacuum away all dust, and wipe the area with a wet sponge. For complete instructions on applying new grout, see pages 76–77 for floors and page 116 for walls.

RECAULKING

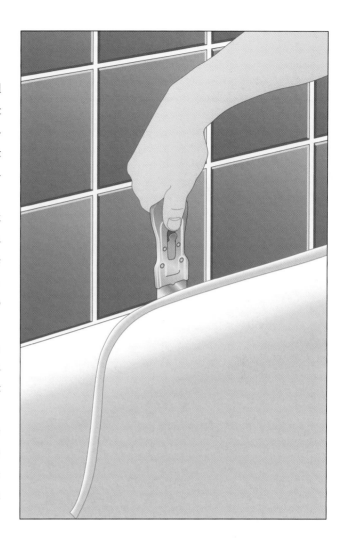

Many bathroom tile installations are marred by a poor caulking job, or by caulking that is stained or peeling. Applying a clean-looking bead of caulk that sticks firmly in place is not easy. Practice on scrap pieces of tile or in an inconspicuous location before you attempt the real thing.

It is imperative that you remove all the old caulk before recaulking. Use a scraping tool that holds a straight razor blade. First scrape down the face of the tiles near the tub, then scrape along the bathtub rim. Next, scrub with an abrasive pad. The tile and the tub should feel smooth.

Some types of caulk can be softened with heat, greatly easing the job of removal. Aim a heat gun or a hair dryer set on high at the caulk until you see it start to change shape, then scrape it away.

Don't scrimp when buying new caulk. Purchase high-quality "tub and tile" caulk, or silicone caulk. To apply a new bead of caulk, choose between the two methods shown on pages 117 and 129.

GROUT COLORANTS

Tile centers carry products that can permanently change the color of grout. Some can even change grout from a darker to a lighter color. To use a grout colorant, clean the grout first, using a special grout cleaner. Apply the colorant with a paint brush or a special applicator, let it soak for the recommended amount of time, and wipe the tiles. It may take two or three coats to achieve the color you desire. Grout colorants are powerful stains, so consult with a tile dealer before coloring grout if the tiles are at all porous.

GROUT HAZE

If grout is not rinsed completely off the tile surfaces during installation and the tiles are porous, a stubborn haze is the result. To clean this away, first allow the grout a full month to completely cure. Then try scrubbing with full-strength white vinegar.

If that doesn't do the trick, wet the area with water. Wearing protective gloves and eye wear, mix five parts water to one part muriatic acid. Scrub the tiles, then rinse several times with clean water. If the haze is still present, try a stronger acid solution.

REMOVING STAINS

If grout or porous tiles are stained, first try scrubbing with a standard cleaning product, and proceed to harsher methods only if that does not work. Apply the recommended product, then scrub with a bristle brush or a fiberglass mesh pad. Be sure to rinse the area clean afterwards; cleaners can cause damage if left in place.

If you have a stubborn stain in a small area, try making a poultice. Mix dry ingredients (such as laundry detergent) with just enough water to make a paste. Scrub the area with the paste, and cover it with a damp cloth for a day or two. Then rinse away paste with clean water.

STAIN REMOVAL

STAIN	SOLUTION
Ink, food stains, or drink stains including coffee	First try hydrogen peroxide, then laundry bleach.
Oil-based stains, paint, tar, or nail polish	First try mineral spirits, then paint remover.
Rust	Scrub in rust remover, then wash with household cleaner.
Dried latex paint	Use a product made to remove latex paint, or lacquer thinner.
White mineral deposits	Brush on a lime-deposit cleaner.

ATTACHING TO WALL TILE OR STONE

Many towel racks, soap dispensers, and other amenities have mounting hardware that attaches with screws. For the strongest hold, use a stud finder to locate a stud or other framing member. Use a masonry bit to drill holes through the tiles (see steps 1 and 2); the holes must be wider than the shank of the screw, or the tile may crack. Then drive long screws into the stud or framing member. Alternatively, install plastic anchors, as shown in steps 2 and 3. They are not very strong, but that can be an advantage. If someone leans heavily on a towel rack, for instance, the anchors will pull out before the tile cracks.

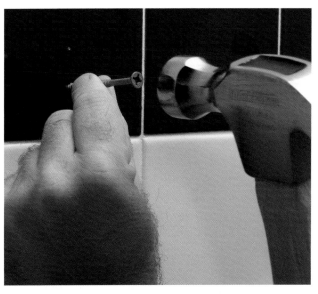

1 **Slightly chip the surface**
Mark for the location of the holes using a felt-tipped pen. Hold the tip of a screw or nail on the exact spot for each hole, and gently tap with a hammer until you have chipped away a slight indentation. This will keep the drill bit from wandering when you bore the hole.

2 **Drill the hole**
Use a masonry drill bit that is the correct size for your plastic anchors. Press the tip of the bit on the indentation, and drill the hole. Hold the drill steady as you drill; moving from side to side could crack a tile.

3 **Tap in the anchor**
Push the plastic anchor into the hole, then tap lightly until it is flush with the surface of the tile. You can now drive a screw into the anchor.

A GUIDE TO CHOOSING AND INSTALLING TILE

TILE AND CHARACTERISTICS	INSTALLATION AND CARE
Cement-body Strong but porous; many types are easily stained and scratched. Almost any color.	Make all cuts with a wet saw. Set in latex-reinforced thinset mortar. Depending on the type, you may need to seal both before and after installing.
Cork Naturally resilient, with a dotted appearance. With regular waxing, these can be very long-lasting.	Cut with a utility knife. Set in special cork tile adhesive, and wax or seal the tile immediately.
Glass Impervious to stains and moisture. Some glass tiles are strong enough for floors, but most are used on walls. Expensive, so they are often used for accents only. A wide variety of textures and colors.	Cut with a snap cutter. Consult with the tile dealer to determine whether to use white organic mastic, white latex-reinforced thinset mortar, or epoxy mortar. Epoxy grout may be needed.
Glazed ceramic (floor) Glazed surface usually very water-resistant; tile itself usually impervious or vitreous. Almost any color and texture.	Make straight cuts with a snap cutter; cutouts with a wet saw or nibbling tool. Set in latex-reinforced thinset mortar.
Glazed ceramic (wall) Typically soft and nonvitreous; covered with a glaze that resists water but may be easily scratched. Virtually all colors. You can install floor tile on a wall, but never install wall tile on a floor.	Make straight cuts with a snap cutter, cutouts with a wet saw or nibbling tool. Set in organic mastic, or in latex-reinforced thinset mortar if the wall will often get wet. Caulk inside corners. All grout lines should be completely filled.
Hardwood Durable and resistant to water, but more easily scratched than ceramic tile; made of wood infused with resin. Woodsy and pastel colors with streaks and mottles.	Cut with a circular saw or table saw. Set in latex-reinforced thinset mortar, and fill joints with latex-reinforced grout.
Laminate See the tile form of laminate strip flooring. The surface is strong and easy to keep clean with little or no maintenance.	Cut with a circular or saber saw. Lay foam backing, then glue the tiles to each other only—not to the floor.
Limestone Very soft, easily stained. Like the limestone found on building façades, limestone tiles and slabs are rough and pitted. Some are cut precisely and some are not.	Make all cuts with a wet saw. Set in latex-reinforced thinset mortar. When installing large pieces on a wall, support the pieces while the mortar sets. Seal before and after installing.

TILE AND CHARACTERISTICS	INSTALLATION AND CARE
Metal Strong enough to be used on floors. Colors depend on the type of metal—typically, copper, brass, stainless steel, or iron. Expensive, so they are usually used as accents.	Plan the installation so you do not have to cut these tiles. Consult with the tile dealer to find out whether to set them in latex-reinforced or epoxy mortar.
Mexican saltillos Very soft and almost sponge-like in their ability to soak up water. May come with a glaze, which can also be prone to staining. Reds, browns, and dark yellow.	Make all cuts with a wet saw. Set in a thick bed of thinset or medium-bed mortar. Because tiles are irregular, set using a 9-tile grid rather than spacers. Seal before and after installing.
Mosaic Individual tiles range from ¾ inch to 4 inches square; sheets are usually 12 inches square. Tiles may be glazed ceramic, marble, or granite. Decorative patterns, already assembled on mosaic sheets, are available.	Cut backing of mosaic sheets with a knife as needed for fit. Set in latex-modified thinset mortar; use white mortar if the tiles are marble. For walls, use organic mastic. Take extra care to make sure all tiles are embedded in the mortar.
Onyx Soft and porous; subject to stains and scratches. Natural stone with distinctive tan and brown swirls.	Make all cuts with a wet saw. Set in white latex-fortified thinset mortar. To resist staining, apply sealer before and after grouting.
Polished granite Very hard and strong. Resistant to scratches and impervious; well-suited for countertops and floors. Speckled, with colors ranging from very light to very dark.	Make all cuts with a wet saw. Set in latex-reinforced thinset mortar.
Polished marble Usually very soft; scratches easily and soaks up water and stains. Distinctive veined patterns with a wide range of colors.	Make all cuts with a wet saw. Exposed edges should be polished, or sanded smooth and painted with clear lacquer. Set in white latex-reinforced thinset mortar. Usually, these tiles are set with the narrowest of grout lines.
Porcelain Impervious or vitreous. Extremely resistant to stains. Can mimic the look and texture of glazed ceramic, polished marble, and even rough stone.	Usually, cut with a wet saw; a nibbling tool may work for cutouts. Set in latex-reinforced thinset mortar.
Quarry Semi-vitreous or vitreous. Prone to staining unless protected by a sealer. Earth tones, gray, or pastel colors.	Cut with a wet saw or make straight cuts with a snap cutter and cutouts with a nibbling tool. Set in latex-reinforced thin-set mortar. To resist staining, apply sealer before grouting.

TILE AND CHARACTERISTICS	INSTALLATION AND CARE
Slate Hard and resistant to scratches and staining. Gray, green, black, and ruddy brown colors. Most slate tiles are made by splitting rather than cutting, so the surface is textured. Some types are polished, and others are left rough.	Make all cuts with a wet saw. Set in latex-reinforced thinset mortar. If the slate is unpolished, seal it before and after installing to protect against stains.
Surface-printed self-adhesive Soft and flexible, requiring very smooth floor substrate. Thin resilient tile stamped with a pattern. The surface is "no-wax," but needs to be renewed if traffic is heavy. Cushioned types are easily damaged.	Cut with a utility knife. Can install without adhesive, but better to use vinyl adhesive to ensure a strong bond.
Terra-cotta Usually nonvitreous; soaks up water and stains readily unless sealed. A range of earth tones, reflecting the color of the clay.	Make all cuts with a wet saw. Set in latex-reinforced thinset mortar. For irregularly shaped types, back-butter each tile as you install it, and use a grid rather than spacers.
Travertine Almost as easily scratched and stained as marble. Small and large pits in the surface may or may not be filled with a light-colored grout. Shades of tan.	Make all cuts with a wet saw. Set in white latex-reinforced thinset mortar, and avoid grouts that can stain. For protection against stains, seal after installing.
Tumbled, honed, resplit, sand-blasted marble and granite Sponge-like texture, prone to staining. Same colors as polished marble or granite.	Make all cuts with a wet saw. Set in white latex-reinforced thinset mortar, and avoid grouts that can stain. Seal the tiles before and after installing.
Vinyl, vinyl composition Soft enough to show underlying irregularities; floor substrate can be flexible, but must be smooth. Resilient, covered with flecks of color to hide dirt. Often called commercial tile, but by combining colors you can achieve an attractive floor. Many types are pre-waxed.	Cut with a knife. Spread vinyl composition adhesive; allow it to dry, then set the tiles.
Wood parquet Needs to be protected with wax or polyurethane finish, but will still buckle if the floor gets very wet; easily scratched. Made of strips of natural wood, usually oak or birch; stains range from dark mahogany to a light maple color.	Cut with a circular saw or other wood-cutting saw. Set in special wood-parquet adhesive.

PHOTOGRAPHY CREDITS

Left (L), Center (C), Right (R), Top (T), Middle (M), Bottom (B)

Unless otherwise credited, all photographs are by **Wayne Cable.**

Russell Abraham: 1, 8 T, 28 B, 46, 48 T, 80, 103, 139 T, 141, 144, 157 B; **Jean Allsopp/Southern Living:** 175; **Marion Brenner:** 135, 136, 137, 162; **James Carrier:** 4, 5, 10, 11, 13 B, 14 B, 15, 17 B, 18 T, 19 BR, 20 B, 21 T, 24 B, 25, 26, 27, 30 B, 31, 33, 177, 183, 184; **Jared Chandler:** 29 TL, 30 T, 99 B, 145 B; **Darien Davis:** 95 T, 101; **Chris Eden:** 19 T; **Fireclay Tile:** 3 BL, 8 B, 22 T, 23 B; **Jay Graham:** 163 B; **Steven Gunther:** 161 B; **Ken Gutmaker:** 24 T; **Jamie Hadley:** 9, 53 B, 102 B; **Margot Hartford:** 139 BL, 142; **Philip Harvey:** 14 T, 19 BL, 44, 96 B, 158 B, 159; **Douglas Johnson:** 29 R, 47 B, 50 T, 78 B, 99 T, 119, 134; **davidduncanlivingston.com:** 47 T, 48 B, 53 T, 95 BL, 96 T, 97, 98, 100 B, 139 BR, 153; **Ron Luxemburg:** 3 T; **Kathryn MacDonald:** 20 T; **Peter Malinowski/InSite:** 7 T; **E. Andrew McKinney:** 13 T, 16, 27 TL, 45 BR, 78 T, 118, 140 T, 143 B, 145 T; **Terrence Moore:** 155 T, 158 T, 161 T, 163 T; **Eric O'Connell:** 18 B, 45 T; **Gary W. Parker:** 156; **Courtesy of Pergo:** 21 B, 52; **David Phelps:** 6, 7 BL, 22 B, 28 T, 45 BL, 49, 109, 114 B, 130, 138, 140 B; **Norman A. Plate:** 157 T, 176; **Buddy Rhodes Studio:** 12 T; **Courtesy of Ann Sacks:** 23 T, 51, 95 BR, 111; **Thomas J. Story:** 160; **Tim Street-Porter:** 94; **Tim Street-Porter/beateworks.com:** 7 BR, 17 T, 50 B, 100 T, 102 T, 155 B, 174, 189; **David Wakely:** 2 L, 143 T; **Deidra Walpole:** 154

Molly McGowan: 27 TL; **Miller-Hull Architects:** 19 T; **Ruben S. Ojeda:** 3 T; **Carolyn E. Oliver-Broder:** 16 T; **Aston Pereira:** 46; **Pergo:** 21, 52; **Frank Perrino & Laura Smith-LAX:** 154; **Brad Polvorosa:** 96 B; **Poster-Frost Associates:** 155 T; **Jeanese Rowell Design:** 118; **David Ruffin:** 141; **Ann Sacks:** 23 T, 51, 95 BR, 111; **Carol Shawn:** 48 T; **Janice Stone, Thomas/Stone Design:** 19 BL; **Talon Architects:** 119 T; **Michael Trahan Interior Design:** 78 B, 134; **Paulette Trainor:** 78 T; **Bernard Trainor Design Associates:** 160; **Jeffrey Trent, Natural Order:** 161 B; **Van-Martin Rowe Design of Pasadena:** 159; **Alison Whittaker:** 103; **Taylor Woodrow:** 44

DESIGNER CREDITS

Alexander Design: 8 T; **Pam Baird:** 80; **Mark Bartos of Hortus Garden/Design:** 158 B; **Bauer Interior Design:** 14 T; **Randi Bernard:** 95 T, 101; **Bianchi Design:** 50 B; **Thomas Bollay, Architect:** 7 T; **Bracken, Arragoni & Ross:** 156; **Debra Buckley Mosaic Tile & Design:** 135-137; **Linda Chase:** 28 T; **Peter Choate:** 158 T; **Susan Churcher:** 18 B, 45 T; **City Studios:** 140 TL; **Color Design Art:** 119 B; **Michael Connell, Architect:** 139 BL, 142; **Dahlin Group Architects:** 99 T; **Kathryne Dahlman:** 53 B; **Esherick, Homsey, Dodge & Davis:** 1; **Bobbie Frohman:** 47 B; **Jan Gardner Interior Design:** 139 T, 144; **Michael Glassman & Associates:** 163 B; **Kay Heizman:** 157 B; **Matthew Henning, Henning/Anderson:** 157 T; **Charles Hess:** 155 BR; **Mary Hoffman:** 163 T; **Gary Hutton Design:** 50 T; **'Idea House' San Francisco Design Center:** 143 B; **Scott Johnson:** 17 T; **Nancy Kintish:** 155 BL; **Macfee & Associates Interior Design:** 53 T, 153; **Leo Marmol & Ron Radziner:** 102 T; **Don Maxcy:** 28 B;

SUPPLIER/MANUFACTURER CREDITS

Chic Tile (650-366-2442): 13 B, 17 B, 30 B; **Fireclay Tile (408-275-1182, www.fireclaytile.com):** 3 BL, 8 B, 22 T, 23 B, 33, cover; **MC Designs (858-689-9596):** 126, 127, 128, 129; **Pergo (1-800-33-PERGO, www.pergo.com):** 21 T, 91; **Quality Discount Tile (650-354-8140):** 150, 151, 152; **Buddy Rhodes Studio (877-706-5303):** 12; **S.D. Hardwood, Inc. (650-631-3976):** 11 B; **Ann Sacks (800-278-8453, www.annsacks.com):** 5, 27, 30 B, 31, 111, 112, 113, 115, 116, 117, 135, 136, 137, cover; **TDM Tiling, Inc. (650-508-0826):** 14 B, 15; **Waterworks (800-899-6757, www.waterworks.com):** 24 B, 26, 31

INDEX